PRINCIPAL COINS
OF THE ROMANS

PRINCIPAL COINS
OF THE ROMANS

VOLUME I
THE REPUBLIC
c.290–31 BC

R.A.G.CARSON

Published for
The Trustees of the British Museum by
British Museum Publications Limited

British Library Cataloguing in Publication Data
Carson, Robert Andrew Glindinning
 The principal coins of the Romans
 Vol. 1: The Republic *c*. 290–31 BC
 1. Coins, Roman
 1. Title 11. British Museum
 737.4'9'37   CJ833

©1978, The Trustees of the British Museum
ISBN 0 7141 0839 1
Published by British Museum Publications Ltd
6 Bedford Square, London WC1B 3RA

Designed by Harry Green
Set in 11 on 12pt Bembo
Printed in Great Britain by Balding and Mansell

Contents

Preface

The Roman Coinage is a vast series which it is difficult to comprehend because of its sheer quantity and its great diversity. These volumes are an attempt to show the growth, development, and changes of the Roman coinage from its inception in the early third century BC to the point in the late fifth century AD when the reforms of Anastasius created a coinage which, in large part, presents obvious differences from the preceding system, and which sets the pattern for the Byzantine coinage.

The Principal Coins of the Romans is divided into three main volumes, the Roman Republic; the Principate, instituted by Augustus at the end of the first century BC and continuing, albeit with considerable modifications to the late third century AD, and, finally, the Dominate which characterised the period from Diocletian to the end of the fifth century AD. Within these main divisions the coinage is arranged in successive chronological groups. A general commentary describing the historical, economic and numismatic circumstances which define and distinguish each group is followed by the detailed description and illustration of the selected coins which, as far as possible are arranged in chronological sequence.

The choice of title was to some extent influenced by that of the Department's very popular *Principal Coins of the Greeks*, first published in 1932, but it will quickly become evident that this book has been conceived along somewhat different lines. The principles which have governed the selection, and the various criteria which were taken into consideration to determine which coins were to be regarded as 'principal' require some elaboration. In general, coins have been selected as 'principal' not simply on grounds such as rarity, importance of association, or artistic distinction, though these, in many instances, were leading factors, but also because they are archetypical pieces which represent the staple coinage at various periods.

Within this general framework coins have been chosen to show the successive monetary systems, the range of denominations comprised in the system with their marks of value or other distinguishing features. Where, in any period, a number of mints were active, coins have been included to illustrate distinctive mint styles, the form of mint signature where such was used, and indications of internal organisation such as officina marks. As far as the resources of the collection permit, at least one portrait is included of every personage of importance for whom coinage was struck, and for the imperial coinage the considerable variety of representation of the imperial bust is illustrated, though not necessarily for each ruler. Since in the rich content of representation on Roman coins the ancient cults for centuries inspired many designs, a comprehensive selection has been included of deities, cult-figures, temples, sacrifice scenes, and processions. The great range of personifications or 'virtues' which are a feature particularly of the imperial coinage also provided a basis for selection. The final major field which has been kept in mind in framing the choice is the wealth of historical reference and illustration which is such a characteristic of Roman coinage throughout practically the whole of its history.

Although rational principles of selection such as those outlined above were applied, inevitably the final choice has been coloured by personal taste and interest, and limited, also, by the necessity to confine the selection within reasonable compass. It is hoped, however, that the selection will present a convenient as well as a comprehensive and comprehensible view of the whole course of Roman coinage.

1 Pre-denarius Coinage
c. 290–212BC

The earliest currency associated with Rome takes the form of rough lumps of bronze, *aes rude*, which required to be weighed to complete a transaction. This was succeeded in time by bronze in the form of bars, initially rough and primitive but gradually developing into a more regular shape and occasionally ornamented with a simple design. Coinage proper begins only in the early third century BC with cast bars of more regular rectangular shape, complete with types on either side, occasionally inscribed, and, at least approximating to a weight standard of five pounds, the so-called *aes signatum*. This coinage is probably associated with the tradition of the first establishment in 289 BC of the board of three moneyers, the *tresviri aere argento auro flando feriundo*.

The next stage brought the introduction of *aes grave*, heavy bronze, still cast but now in circular shape, and of regular though roughly adjusted weight, with a distinctive type on both sides, together with a mark of value. Associated with several series of *aes grave*, produced at a standard of a pound (libra) for the unit, the *as*, were issues of struck silver didrachms, inscribed ROMANO, accompanied by struck token bronze. One series of these didrachms which, because its types have specific reference to Rome and was presumably struck there, is probably to be identified with the Romans' 'first silver' which Pliny dates to 269 BC.

This coinage of didrachms and associated *aes grave* was the coinage of Rome during the First Punic War, but it was replaced about 235 BC

with a new series of didrachms and occasional drachms inscribed ROMA, accompanied still by *aes grave*, initially on the standard of the reduced Latin pound of 272 gm. Three types of these didrachms were short-lived, being discontinued probably about 227 BC, but the fourth, with types of young Janus head and quadriga, was still in issue at the outbreak of the Second Punic War in 218 BC. Rome's first gold coinage of staters with a similar young Janus obverse and an oath-scene reverse was issued early in this war about 216 BC. The cast *aes grave*, chiefly the series associated with Rome itself, with Janus head on obverse of the *as* and other deities on lower denominations but with a consistent prow reverse, underwent successive reductions in weight. By about 220 BC the initial standard, which had been falling, was replaced by a semi-libral standard for the *as* unit, but only a few years later about 216 BC the *as* weight had fallen to a post semi-libral standard of 88 gm.

---

1   Half-litra *c.* 300 BC

Obv. Head of Apollo r.
Rev. Fore-part of man-headed bull r.; above, *ΡΩΜΑΙΩΝ* . Struck Æ, 2.66 gm. ←.
This, the earliest coin with explicit mention of Rome, copies the types of bronze coins of Naples.

2

3

2   **Bronze bar** *c.* 280 BC
Obv. Eagle with outspread wings, facing,
     head r., and holding thunderbolt.
Rev. Pegasus galloping l.; below, ROMANOM.
     Cast Æ, 1390.03 gm.
Rare instance of an inscribed bar.

3   **Bronze bar** *c.* 274 BC
Obv. Elephant r.
Rev. Sow l. Cast Æ, 1746.47 gm.
A reference to the Romans' first encounter
with the war-elephant in the war with Pyrrhus
of Epirus, and possibly specifically to the

tradition that in one battle the elephants of Pyrrhus were frightened by the grunting of swine on the Roman side. *cf.* Aelian, *De natura animalium*, I. XXXVIII.

4   Didrachm *c.* 280 BC

Obv. Head of Mars, helmeted, l.
Rev. Horse's head, with bridle, r.; to l., Corn-ear; on tablet below, ROMANO. Æ, 7.56 gm. ↙.

5   Half-litra *c.* 280 BC

Obv. Head of Minerva, helmeted, r.; to l., star; below, ROMANO.
Rev. Horse's head, with bridle, l.; around, ROMANO. Struck Æ, 5.90 gm. ↑.

6   *As* *c.* 280 BC

Obv. Head of Janus, diademed; above, mark of value, I.
Rev. Head of Mercury in *petasus* l.; above, mark of value, I. Cast Æ, 330.0 gm. 'Heavy' libral standard.

7   Didrachm *c.* 275 BC

Obv. Head of Apollo, laureate, l.; to l., ROMANO.
Rev. Free horse r.; above, star. Æ, 6.82 gm. ↗.

8   Litra *c.* 275 BC

Obv. Head of Apollo, diademed r.
Rev. Lion walking r., holding in jaws broken spear on which it rests l. paw; in ex., ROMANO. Struck Æ, 7.97 gm.

9   As *c*. 275 BC

Obv. Head of Apollo, diademed r.; above,
    mark of value, I.
Rev. As *obv*., but head l.
    Cast Æ, 295.0 gm. ↑.
'Heavy libral standard.

10   Didrachm *c*. 269 BC

Obv. Head of young Hercules r., wearing
    lion-skin, and with club on r. shoulder.
Rev. She-wolf, standing r., suckling the
    twins, Romulus and Remus.
    Æ, 7.92 gm.
The types of Hercules and wolf and twins
contain allusions to Fabius and Ogulnius who
were consuls at Rome in 269 BC.

11   Dupondius *c.* 269 BC

Obv. Head of Diana, in crested helmet, r.; to
l., mark of value, II.
Rev. Wheel of six spokes, between two of
which, mark of value, II.
Cast Æ, 600.24 gm.
'Heavy' libral standard.

12   Didrachm *c.* 265 BC

Obv. Head of Diana, wearing helmet with
gryphon crest, r.; to l., symbol, dog.
Rev. Victory standing r.; holding palm
branch with wreath attached; to r.;
ROMANO, to l., K. AR, 6.75 gm. ↓.

13   Double-litra *c.* 265 BC

Obv. Head of Diana, wearing helmet with
gryphon crest, l.; to l., ROMANO.
Rev. Eagle, with upraised wings, standing l.
on thunderbolt; around, ROMANO.
Struck Æ, 15.29 gm. ↓.

14   As *c.* 260 BC

Obv. Head of Minerva, wearing helmet with
three crests, facing.
Rev. Bull walking r., head facing; above, ⌐;
in ex. ROMA. Æ, 292.09 gm. ↑.
'Heavy' libral standard.

15   Didrachm 235–227 BC

Obv. Head of Mars, in crested helmet ornamented with gryphon, r.,
Rev. Horse's head, with bridle, r.; to r.,
symbol, sickle; below, ROMA.
Æ, 6.61 gm.

16   Drachm 235–227 BC

Obv. As No. 15, but without gryphon
ornament.
Rev. As No. 15. Æ, 2.88 gm. ←.

17   Didrachm 235–227 BC

Obv. Head of Apollo, laureate, r.
Rev. Free horse l.; above, ROMA.
Æ, 6.38 gm. ↑.

18   Drachm 235–227 BC

Obv. As No. 17.
Rev. As No. 17. Æ, 3.28 gm. ↙.

19   Didrachm 235–227 BC

Obv. Head of Mars, in crested helmet, r.; to
l., symbol, club.
Rev. Free horse l.; above, symbol, club;
below, ROMA. Æ, 6.01 gm. ↘.

20   Half-litra 235–227 BC

Obv. Head of Apollo, laureate, r.
Rev. Horse, with bridle l.; below, ROMA.
Struck Æ, 3.95 gm. ↘.

21   Quarter-litra 235–227 BC

Obv. Head of Diana, wearing helmet with
gryphon crest, r.; to l., symbol, club.
Rev. Dog r.; in ex., ROMA.
Struck Æ, 1.79 gm. ↓.

22   As *c.* 235 BC

Obv. Head of Diana, wearing helmet with
gryphon crest, r.; to l., symbol, club.
Rev. As *obv.*, but head l.
Cast Æ, 291.05 gm. ↑.
'Light' libral standard.

23   Didrachm 235 BC

Obv. Head of young Janus, laureate.
Rev. Jupiter, hurling thunderbolt with r. hand
     and holding sceptre in l., in quadriga r.,
     driven by Victory; on tablet below,
     ROMA incuse. Æ, 6.63 gm. ↓.

24   Drachm *c.* 225 BC

Obv. As No. 23.
Rev. As No. 23, but quadriga l.; in ex, ROMA.
     Æ, 3.33 gm. ↓.

25   Didrachm *c.* 216 BC

Obv. As No. 23.
Rev. As No. 23, but below, symbol, corn-ear,
     and, on tablet, ROMA in relief.
     Æ, 6.67 gm. ←.

26   As *c.* 235 BC.

Obv. Head of Janus, bearded; below, mark of
     value, I.
Rev. Prow r.; above, mark of value, I. Cast Æ,
     253.19 gm. ↖.
'Reduced' libral standard.

27   **As** *c.* 235 BC.

Obv. As No. 26, but no mark of value.
Rev. Prow l.; above, mark of value, I. Cast Æ,
       258.06 gm. ↑.
'Reduced' libral standard.

28   **Semis** *c.* 235 BC

Obv. Head of Jupiter, laureate l.; below, mark
       of value, s.
Rev. Prow r.; above, mark of value, s. Cast
       Æ, 140.44 gm. ↑.
'Reduced' libral standard.

29 Triens *c.* 235 BC

Obv. Head of Minerva, wearing Corinthian
helmet, l.; below, mark of value, **· · · ·**
Rev. Prow r.; below, mark of value, **· · · ·**
Cast Æ, 93.84 gm. ↑.
'Reduced' libral standard.

30 Quadrans *c.* 235 BC

Obv. Head of Hercules, wearing lion-skin, l.;
below, mark of value, **· · ·**
Rev. Prow r.; below, mark of value, **· · ·**
Cast Æ, 73.43 gm.
'Reduced' libral standard.

31 Sextans *c.* 235 BC

Obv. Head of Mercury, wearing petasus, l.;
below, mark of value, **· ·**
Rev. Prow r.; below, mark of value, **· ·** Cast
Æ, 53.65 gm. ↑.
'Reduced' libral standard.

32 Uncia *c.* 235 BC

Obv. Head of Roma, wearing crested
Athenian helmet, l.; to r., mark of
value, **·**
Rev. Prow r., below, mark of value, **·** Cast
Æ, 20.48 gm. ↑.
'Reduced' libral standard.

20

36

33   Didrachm *c.* 216 BC

Obv. As No. 23.
Rev. As No. 23, but on tablet below, ROMA in
relief. Æ, 6.45 gm. ←.

34   Stater *c.* 216 BC

Obv. Head of young Janus, laureate.
Rev. A youth kneeling between two warriors
who touch with swords a pig which the
youth holds; each warrior holds spear in
left hand; in ex, ROMA. Ν, 6.88 gm. ↘.

35   Half-stater *c.* 216 BC

Obv. As No. 34.
Rev. As No. 34. Ν, 3.41 gm. ↓.

36   Decussis *c.* 216 BC
Obv. Head of Diana, wearing Phrygian
helmet with gryphon crest, r.; to l., x.
Rev. Prow l,; above, x. Cast Æ, 640.0 gm. ↑.
Post semi-libral standard.

37   Dupondius *c.* 216 BC

Obv. Head of Minerva, wearing crested
Corinthian helmet, r.; to l.; mark of
value, II.
Rev. Prow l.; above, mark of value, II.
Cast Æ, 185.52 gm. ↑.
Post semi-libral standard.

38   **As** c. 216 BC

Obv. Head of Janus.
Rev. Prow l.; above, mark of value, I.
      Cast Æ, 90.76 gm. ↑.
Post semi-libral standard.

39   **Triens** c. 216 BC

Obv. Head of Minerva, wearing crested
      Corinthian helmet, l.; below, mark of
      value, ● ● ●.
Rev. Prow l.; below, mark of value, ● ● ●.
      Cast Æ, 37.62 gm. ↑.
Post semi-libral standard.

40   **Triens** c. 216 BC

Obv. As No. 39, but head r., and above,
      ROMA.
Rev. Prow r., below, mark of value, ● ● ● ●;
      above, ROMA. Struck Æ, 24.73 gm. →.
Post semi-libral standard.

41   **Quartuncia** c. 216 BC

Obv. Head of Roma, wearing crested
      Athenian helmet, r.
Rev. Prow r.; above, ROMA.
      Struck Æ, 2.35 gm. ↑.
Post semi-libral standard.

42   **Uncia** *c.* 220 BC

Obv. Head of Sol facing, radiate; to l., mark
       of value, •.
Rev. Crescent enclosing two stars; above,
       mark of value, •; below, ROMA.
       Struck Æ, 13.02 gm. ←.
This coin is part of a series, distinct from the
prow series, of semi-libral standard, restricted
to denominations from triens to uncia, and all
struck.

43   **Sextans** *c.* 215 BC

Obv. Head of Mercury, wearing petasus, r.;
        to l., mark of value, ••.
Rev. Prow r.; above, corn-ear and ROMA;
       below, mark of value, ••.
       Struck Æ, 7.58 gm. ↓.
'Light' post semi-libral standard. Uncertain
local mint.

2 Denarius Coinage
c. 211–125 BC

The straits to which Rome had been reduced by Hannibal's invasion of Italy are reflected in the successive reductions of the weight standard of the *aes grave* coinage and the reduction in both weight and fineness of the quadrigatus didrachm in the opening years of the Second Punic War. Revived confidence and restored resources are, however, evident in the introduction of a new coinage which on the archaeological evidence from Morgantina must have been carried out by 211 BC. The essence of the new coinage was the creation of the silver denarius which was to remain the staple Roman coin for something like four centuries. This coin of a nominal value of ten *asses* was struck initially at a weight of 4.50 gm., falling eventually to 3.90 gm. It was supplemented in silver by a half-piece, the quinarius of five *asses*, and the sestertius of two and a half *asses*. The companion series of bronze coins included denominations from *as* down to semuncia, all of which were now struck, not cast. At the point where the denarius was introduced the bronze coins were of sextantal standard, the *as* having a weight of 55 gm., but quite soon the standard slipped even further until the *as* was struck at an uncial standard, a weight of 27 gm.

Probably somewhere about 211 BC appeared a new coinage in gold in denominations of 60, 40, and 20 *asses*. The silver denarius was Rome's new universal silver denomination, but a second series of silver coins now also appeared, the victoriate, so termed from its types of Jupiter head and Victory crowning trophy. From its weight standard, initially of 3.40 gm. falling to 2.90 gm. it seems to have been the extension of the reduced quadrigatus didrachm, and a replacement for local issues in silver of this approximate standard. The victoriate, initially issued in quantity, and probably from a variety of mints, continued with a decreasing frequency until its disappearance before the middle of the second century BC.

The issues of the denarius with types of Roma head and the Dioscuri, at first anonymous, soon acquired distinguishing features in the form of a symbol or a monogram. By about 175 BC these gave way to a fairly full form of the name of the moneying magistrate and shortly after this there appeared a new reverse of Diana in biga of horses. The monopoly of the Dioscuri reverse was further broken about the middle of the century by the first use of special reverse types alluding to events, real or legendary, in the earlier history of the moneyers' families and over the next two decades was largely replaced by reverses of a great variety of deities in chariots. On the obverse, also, representations other than the standard Roma head began to appear. In the second half of the century, also, the value mark on the denarius, X, for ten *asses*, was replaced by XVI, very soon abbreviated to ✗.

44   **Denarius** *c.* 211 BC

Obv. Head of Roma, helmeted, r.; behind
head, mark of value, x.
Rev. The Dioscuri on horseback, charging r.,
each holding spear; above, two stars;
below, on tablet, ROMA.
Æ, 4.11 gm. ←.
The Dioscuri who, according to legend, had
come to the aid of Rome at the battle of Lake
Regillus in 497 BC form an apt type for the new
coinage in the crisis of the war against
Hannibal.

45   **Quinarius** *c.* 211 BC

Obv. As No. 44, but mark of value, v.
Rev. As No. 44. Æ, 2.24 gm. →.

46   **Sestertius** *c.* 211 BC

Obv. As No. 44, but mark of value,**IIS**.
Rev. As No. 44. Æ, 1.07 gm. ←.

47   **As** *c.* 211 BC

Obv. Head of Janus laureate; above, mark of
value, I.
Rev. Prow r.; above, mark of value, I;
below, ROMA. Æ, 32.43 gm. ↙.

48   **Semis** *c.* 211 BC

Obv. Head of Jupiter, laureate, r.; to l., mark
of value, s.
Rev. Prow r.; above, mark of value, s;
below, ROMA. Æ, 18.60 gm. ↙.

49   **Triens** *c.* 211 BC

Obv. Head of Minerva, helmeted, r.; above
mark of value, • • • •.
Rev. Prow r., above. ROMA; below, mark of
value, • • • •. Æ, 12.31 gm. →.

50   Quadrans *c.* 211 BC

Obv. Head of Hercules in lion skin head-dress,
r.; to l., mark of value, **. . .** .
Rev. Prow r., above, ROMA; below, mark of
value, **. . .** Æ, 10.11 gm.

51   Sextans *c.* 211 BC

Obv. Bust of Mercury in winged *petasus*
draped, r.; above, mark of value, **. .** .
Rev. Prow r.; above, ROMA; below, mark of
value, **. .** Æ, 6.16 gm. ↓.

52   Uncia *c.* 211 BC

Obv. Head of Roma, helmeted, r.; to l., mark
of value, **.** .
Rev. Prow r., above, ROMA; below mark of
value, **.** Æ 3.95 gm. ↑.

53   Semuncia *c.* 211 BC

Obv. Bust of Mercury, in winged *petasus*,
draped, r.
Rev. Prow r.; above, ROMA. Æ, 2.40 gm. ↖.

54   Sixty asses *c.* 209 BC

Obv. Bust of Mars, helmeted, draped, r.; to l.,
mark of value, ↓X.
Rev. Eagle, with out-stretched wings, standing on thunderbolt, r.; below, ROMA.
N, 3.41 gm. →.

55   Forty asses *c.* 209 BC

Obv. As No. 54, but mark of value, XXXX.
Rev. As No. 54. N, 2.23 gm. ↓.

56   Twenty asses *c.* 209 BC

Obv. As No. 55, but mark of value, XX.
Rev. As No. 54. N, 1.13 gm. ↗.

57   Forty asses *c.* 209 BC

Obv. As No. 55.
Rev. As No. 54, but above, symbol, staff.
N, 3.34 gm. ↓.

58 Victoriate *c.* 211–200 BC

Obv. Head of Jupiter, laureate, r.; below, N.
Rev. Victory standing r.; placing wreath on
trophy of arms; in ex., ROMA.
ᴁ, 3.28 gm. →.
N on obverse may indicate a mint in South
Italy.

59 Victoriate 211–200 BC

Obv. Head of Jupiter, laureate, r.
Rev. Victory standing r., placing wreath on
trophy of arms; in field, centre, ᴁ, and
right, ᴧ; in ex., ROMA. ᴁ, 2.77 gm. ←.
Minted in Corcyra.

60 Victoriate 211–200 BC

Obv. Head of Jupiter, laureate, r.
Rev. Victory standing r., placing wreath on
trophy of arms; in field, centre, CROT; in
ex. ROMA. ᴁ, 3.25 gm. ←.
Minted at Croton.

61 Half-victoriate 211–200 BC

Obv. Head of Mars, helmeted, r., below, ᴸ.
Rev. Horseman l.; below, T; to r. to r. [s]; in
ex., ROMA. ᴁ, 1.65 gm. ↗.
South Italy.

62 Half-victoriate 211–200 BC

Obv. Head of Jupiter, laureate, r.
Rev. Victory standing r., placing wreath on
trophy of arms; in field, centre, ᴃ, and
to right, s; in ex. ROMA.
ᴁ, 1.28 gm. ↘.
Minted at Vibo.

63 Quinarius 211–200 BC

Obv. As No. 45.
Rev. As No. 45, but below, to r., C.
ᴁ, 2.24 gm. ↗.
The initial C represents a mint in Sardinia, for
bronzes of this group are found overstruck on
Sardinian bronzes

64   Denarius 211–200 BC

Obv. As No. 44.
Rev. As No. 44, but above, to l., symbol,
Victory with wreath. Æ, 4.25 gm. ←.
One of the earliest issues with distinguishing
symbol, here placed unusually in upper field.

65   Denarius 211–200 BC

Obv. As No. 44.
Rev. As No. 44, but below, symbol,
caduceus. Æ, 4.46 gm. ↑.

66   Denarius 211–200 BC

Obv. As No. 44.
Rev. As No. 44, but below, monogram, ℞.
Æ, 4.36 gm. ↑.
Specific indication of mintage at Rome.

67   Denarius 211–200 BC

Obv. As No. 44.
Rev. As No. 44, but below, B. Æ, 4.25 gm. ↙.
The B may indicate a mint at Beneventum.

68   Denarius 200–175 BC

Obv. As No. 44.
Rev. As No. 44, but below, C. ÂL.
Æ, 4.41 gm. ↑.
An early instance of a monogram of the name
of the moneying magistrate C. Allius.

69   Dupondius 200–175 BC

Obv. Head of Minerva, helmeted, r.
Rev. Prow, r.; above, mark of value II.
Æ, 47.61 gm. ↑.
Uncial standard. Overstruck on an *as* of the
sexantal standard.

70   As 200–175 BC

Obv. Head of Janus, laureate; above, mark of
value, I; below C𝖠.
Rev. Prow r.; above, mark of value, I;
below, ROMA. Æ, 21.38 gm. ↓.
Uncial standard.

71 Dextans 200–175 BC

Obv. Head of Ceres, with corn-wreath, r.
Rev. Victory in quadriga r.; above, ʟ below, ROMA; in ex., S ⹁ • • • • . Æ, 12.05 gm. ←.
Uncial standard. An example of a rare denomination, ten unciae. The letter ʟ may indicate a mint in Luceria.

72 Quincunx 200–175 BC

Obv. Head of Apollo, laureate, r.; to l.; ⌐.
Rev. The Dioscuri on horseback r.; above, two stars; below, ROMA; in ex. • • • • • . Æ, 7.45 gm. ↘.
An unusual denomination, five unciae. The mint indicated by the letter, ⌐ has been tentatively suggested as Palio in South Italy.

73 Denarius 200–175 BC

Obv. As No. 44.
Rev. As No. 44, but below, QLC.
   ÆR, 4.24 gm. ↖.
Moneyer: Q. Lutatius Cerco (?).

74 Denarius 200–175 BC

Obv. As No. 44.
Rev. As No. 44, but below, A͡L.
   ÆR, 3.90 gm. ↘.
Same moneyer as No. 68 above at another mint.

75 Denarius 200–175 BC

Obv. As No. 44.
Rev. As No. 44, but below, sx.Q.
   ÆR, 4.02 gm. ↖.
Uncertain mint.
Moneyer: Sextus Quinctilius (?).

76 Stater *c.* 197 BC

Obv. Bare head of Flamininus, bearded, r.
Rev. Victory standing l.; holding wreath and palm; to l.; T. QUINCTI. Ν, 8.42 gm. ↑.
A rare series of coins was struck in Greece by or in honour of T. Quinctius Flamininus after his defeat of Philip V of Macedon at Cynoscephalae. The types are adapted from those of the traditional Macedonian stater whose Athena head obverse is replaced by a portrait of Flamininus. This is the first instance of the portrait of a living Roman to appear on coinage.

77   Denarius *c.* 175 BC

Obv. As No. 44.
Rev. Diana in biga of horses, r.; below, on
tablet, ROMA, and symbol, prawn.
Æ, 3.92 gm. ←.
An early example of the replacement of the
traditional Dioscuri reverse of the denarius.

78   Sextans *c.* 175 BC

Obv. Bust of Mercury in winged petasus, r.;
above, mark of value, • •.
Rev. Prow r.; above, symbol, small figure of
Ulysses; to r.; mark of value, • •;
below, ROMA. Æ, 6.70 gm. ←.
Uncial standard. An instance from a period of
coinage when the moneyers issued bronze only
without accompanying silver.
Moneyer: L. Mamilius.

79   Denarius 175–150 BC

Obv. As No. 44.
Rev. No. 44, but below, C.IVNI.C.F.
Æ, 3.43 gm. ↗.
An early example of the moneyer's name in
fuller form.
Moneyer. C. Junius.

80   Denarius 175–150 BC

Obv. As No. 44 but to the l., PITIO, to r., mark
of value, X.
Rev. As No. 44, but below, L.SEMP.
Æ, 3.71 gm. →.
The moneyer's name, L. Sempronius Pitio,
begins on the reverse and is completed on the
obverse.

81   Denarius 175–150 BC

Obv. As No. 44, but also to l., symbol,
Victory.
Rev. As No. 44, but below, C.TER.LVC.
Æ, 4.04 gm. →.
Unusual use of symbol on obverse in addition
to moneyer's name, C. Terentius Lucanus, on
the reverse.

82   Denarius *c.* 150 BC

Obv. Head of Roma, helmeted, r.; to l., mark
of value, X and TI·VET.
Rev. Kneeling youth holding a pig, and
flanked by two warriors, each holding
spear and touching the pig with their
swords; above, ROMA. Æ, 3.96 gm. →.
A reminiscence of the reverse type of the gold
stater, No. 34 above.
Moneyer: Ti Veturius.

83   Denarius *c.* 150 BC

Obv. Head of Roma, helmeted, r.; below
    chin, mark of value, x.
Rev. She-wolf standing r., suckling the twins,
    Romulus and Remus; behind, fig-tree
    with three birds; to l., the shepherd
    Faustulus holding staff in l. hand;
    around, SEX. POM. FOSTLVS.
    Æ, 3.94 gm. ↖.

The moneyer, Sextus Pompeius Fostlus,
claimed descent from Faustulus, the shepherd
who, according to legend, found the twins
being suckled by the wolf. An early instance of
the use of reverse types, alluding to events in
the early history of the moneyer's family.

84   Denarius 150–125 BC

Obv. Head of Roma, helmeted, r.; below,
    mark of value, x.
Rev. Victory in biga of horses, r., below,
    NATTA and, on tablet, ROMA.
    Æ, 3.50 gm.
Moneyer: Natta.

85   Denarius 150–125 BC

Obv. As No. 85.
Rev. Juno in biga of goats, r.; below, C. RENI;
    in ex., ROMA. Æ, 3.94 gm. ↓.
Moneyer: C. Renius.

86   Denarius 150–125 BC

Obv. As No. 85, but all within laurel-wreath.
Rev. Mars and goddess Nerio, in quadriga of
    horses, r.; below, CN.GEL; in ex., ROMA.
    Æ, 3.72 gm. ↖.
Moneyer: Cn. Gellius.

87   Denarius 150–125 BC

Obv. As No. 85.
Rev. Victory in biga of horses, r.; below,
    C.VAL. C.F, and, on tablet, ROMA; above,
    FLAC. Æ, 3.93 gm. →.
Moneyer. C. Valerius Flaccus.

88   Denarius 150–125 BC

Obv. As No. 85, but to l., mark of value, XVI.
Rev. As No. 87. Æ, 3.79 gm. ↘.

A coin of the same types and moneyer as the
previous piece, but the mark of value now
overtly indicating its tariffing as sixteen *asses*.

89   Denarius 150–125 BC

Obv. Head of Roma, helmeted, r.; to l.,
   ROMA; below chin, mark of value, ✖.
Rev. Victory in quadriga of horses, r.; in ex.,
   C.NVMITORI. ℞, 3.87 gm. ✓.
The mark of value, ✖ is a shortened form of XVI.
Moneyer: C. Numitorius.

90   Denarius 150–125 BC

Obv. Head of Roma, helmeted, r.; to l., mark
   of value, ✖.
Rev. Venus in biga of horses, r.; above, small
   Victory, with wreath, flying l.; below,
   P.CALP; in ex., ROMA. ℞, 3.84 gm. ←.
Struck on large flan.
Moneyer: P. Calpurnius.

91   Denarius 125–100 BC

Obv. Head of Roma, helmeted. r.; to l.,
   laurel-wreath; below, x and ROMA.
Rev. The Dioscuri on horseback galloping in
   opposite directions, looking back, and
   holding spear, point downward; above,
   two stars; in ex., C. SERVEILI. M. F.
      ℞, 4.02 gm. ↘.
Moneyer: C. Serveilius.

92   Denarius 150–125 BC

Obv. Head of Roma, helmeted r.; to l.,
   voting urn, and mark of value ✖.
Rev. Libertas, holding *pileus* and sceptre, in
   quadriga of horses, r.; below, C.CASSI; in
   ex., ROMA. ℞, 3.89 gm. ↖.
Moneyer: C. Cassius.

93   Denarius 150–125 BC

Obv. Head of Roma, helmeted, r.; to l.,
   ROMA; under chin, mark of value, x.
Rev. C.AVG divided by column crowned by
   figure holding sceptre and corn-ears,
   and flanked at base by lion's head
   surmounted by corn-ear; to l., togate
   figure holding dish and loaf and placing
   foot on modius; to r., togate figure
   holding lituus. ℞, 3.86 gm. ✓.
The reverse type alludes to the interest of
earlier members of the moneyer's family in the
corn supply. The column outside the Porta
Trigemina honoured L. Minucius Augurinus
who reduced corn prices in 439 BC.
Moneyer: C. Minucius Augurinus.

94   Denarius 150–125 BC

Obv. As No. 85, but to r., COTA.
Rev. Hercules in biga of centaurs, each with branch over shoulder, r.; below, M. AV̂RELI; on tablet, ROMA. Æ, 3.72 gm. ↗.
Moneyer's name, M. Aurelius Cota, continued on the obverse.

95   Denarius 150–125 BC

Obv. Head of Roma, helmeted, r.; to l., small tripod; below chin, mark of value ✗.
Rev. Apollo, holding bow with arrow strung, in biga of horses, r; below, M. OPEIMI; in ex., ROMA. Æ, 3.90 gm. ↓.
Moneyer: M. Opeimius.

96   Denarius 150–125 BC

Obv. Head of Roma, helmeted r.; to l., anchor; below chin, mark of value, ✗.
Rev. Venus, crowned by cupid, in biga of horses, r.; above, ROMA; below SEX. IV̂LI; in ex., CAISAR. Æ, 3.92 gm. ↖.
The figures of Venus and Cupid on the reverse allude to the Julian family's traditional descent from Julius, grandson of Venus and Anchises.
Moneyer: Sextus Iulius Caesar.

97   Denarius 150–125 BC

Obv. Head of Roma, helmeted, r.; to l., mark of value, ✗.
Rev. Pax, holding branch and sceptre, in biga of horses. r.; below, elephant's head with bell, and ROMA. Æ, 3.82 gm. ↗.
The moneyer may have been a member of the Caecilian family of which the elephant's head was the usual badge.

98   Dodrans 150–125 BC

Obv. Bust of Vulcan, draped, and with laureate *pileus*, r.; to l., pincers, and mark of value S∴.
Rev. Prow r.; to r., mark of value, S∴; above C.CASSI; below, ROMA. Æ, 15.42 gm. ↑.
An extremely rare instance of this denomination of nine unciae or three-quarters of an *as*.
Moneyer: C. Cassius

99   Bes 150–125 BC

Obv. Head of Bacchus, with ivy-wreath, r.; to
       l., mark of value, **S:**.
Rev. As No. 98, but to r., mark of value, **S:**.
       Æ, 9.50 gm. ↑.
This is the only instance of the use of this
denomination of eight *unciae* or two-thirds of
an *as*.
Moneyer: C. Cassius.

3 Denarius Coinage
125–92BC

The coinage of the last quarter of the century and the early years of the next century down to the outbreak of the Social War in 91 BC represents a smooth transition and development from the later issues of the previous period. The precious metal coinage is here in silver only, and where this is accompanied by bronze issues these are of the uncial standard. The line of demarcation between this and the previous period is not very precise, but the denarius coinage of this period witnesses the practical displacement of the head of Roma on the obverse by heads of deities and personifications, and, on the reverse, the disappearance of chariot-borne deities in favour of types containing allusions to events associated with the earlier history of the moneyer's family. The mark of value for most of the period is in the form ✗, though towards the end the traditional form x reappears. The attribution of precise dates to specific issues in this period is difficult, but, on the evidence of hoards, at least the sequence of issues can be determined with reasonable certainty.

100 Denarius 125–100 BC

Obv. Head of Roma, helmeted, r.; to l., lituus; below, ROMA; below chin, ✗.

Rev. Horseman, with shield inscribed M, galloping l., and spearing fleeing horseman armed with spear and shield; in ex., C. SERVEIL. Æ, 3.99 gm. ↑.

On the reverse, the horseman, claimed as an ancestor of the moneyer (C. Serveilius), is identified as M. Servilius Pulex Geminus, said by Plutarch to have been wounded but victorious in twenty-three single combats.

101 Denarius 125–100 BC

Obv. Head of Roma, helmeted, r.; to l., x; below chin, K.

Rev. Q. Fabius Pictor, helmeted, cuirassed, seated l., holding flamen's cap and spear, with, beside him, shield inscribed QVI/RIN; behind head, N; around N. FABI PICTOR; in ex., ROMA. Æ, 3.93 gm. ↑.

Fabius Pictor, appointed praetor in Sardinia in 189 BC was not permitted to take up his appointment as he had been consecrated *flamen quirinalis* in the preceding year. The coin provides an early instance of the use of variable control marks in the form of letters on obverse and reverse.

102 Denarius 125–120 BC

Obv. Head of Roma, helmeted, r.; to l.,
ROMA; below chin, ✗.
Rev. Jupiter, holding thunderbolt, in biga of
elephants, l.; above Victory with
wreath; in ex., C.MĒTELLVS.
Æ, 3.97 gm. →.
In his victory over the Carthaginians at
Panormus in 251 BC L. Caecilius Metellus
captured all their elephants, which later
appeared in his triumph at Rome.
Moneyer: C. Caecilius Metellus.

103 Denarius 125–100 BC

Obv. Head of Janus, laureate; around M.FOVRI.
L.F.
Rev. Roma, helmeted, standing l., holding
sceptre and placing wreath on trophy,
on either side of which a Gallic shield
and carnyx; above Roma, a star; to r.,
ROMA; in ex., PHILI. Æ, 3.98 gm. ←.
A reference to victories over the Gauls in
223 BC of an earlier Furius Philius.
Moneyer: M. Furius Philius.

104 Denarius *c.* 118 BC

Obv. Head of Roma, helmeted, r.; to l.,
ROMA and ✗; to r., M.AVRELI.
Rev. Naked warrior, holding spear, shield,
and carnyx, in biga of horses, r.; below,
SCAVRI; in ex., L.LIC.CN.DOM.
Æ, 3.89 gm. ↓.
The occasion of this coinage was the
foundation of the colony of Narbo Martius
(Narbonne) in Gaul in 118 BC. The founding
commissioners, Licinius and Domitius are
named as well as the moneyer (M. Aurelius
Scaurius). The warrior is probably Bituitus,
king of the Arverni, captured in battle in 121
BC.

105 Quadrans *c.* 110 BC

Obv. Bust of Hercules, draped in lion skin, r.;
above, •••; to r. CN.DOMI.
Rev. Club between bow and arrow; above,
M.SILA; below, Q.CVRTI. Æ, 6.35 gm. ←.
The reverse is a departure from the traditional
prow type.
Moneyers: Cn. Domitius, M. Silanus and
Q. Curtius.

106 Denarius *c.* 110 BC

Obv. Bust of Roma, laureate, draped r.; to l.,
✗; to r., ROMA.
Rev. Equestrian statue on triple arch; around,
MN AEMILIO; in arches, LEP. Æ, 3.91 gm. ↘.
Moneyer: Manius Aemilius Lepidus.

107 Denarius *c.* 105 BC

Obv. Male head, helmeted, r.; to l., caduceus;
above, ✖; to r., CN. BLASIO CN.F.
Rev. Jupiter, holding sceptre and thunderbolt,
standing facing between Juno amd
Minerva; each holds sceptre and
Minerva crowns Jupiter with wreath; in
ex., ROMA. Æ, 3.87 gm.←.
The obverse portrait may be that of Scipio
Africanus; the reverse represents the Capitoline
Triad.
Moneyer: Cn. Cornelius Blasio.

108 As *c.* 105 BC

Obv. Head of Janus, laureate; around, ROMA;
above, I.
Rev. Victory, standing front, head r., placing
helmet on trophy; around and in ex.,
CN.BLASIO CN.F. Æ, 26.88 gm. ←.
New reverse type for the *as*, struck again after
an interval of years.
Moneyer: Cn. Cornelius Blasio.

109 Denarius *c.* 105 BC

Obv. Bust of Veiovis, diademed and with cloak
over shoulder, holding thunderbolt, l.; to
r., ᛗ.
Rev. The two Lares seated r., holding spear
and caressing dog standing between
them; above, head of Vulcan l., with
tongs; in field l., L͡A and r., R͡R; in ex.,
L.CAESI. Æ, 3.93 gm. ←.
A possible connection with Rhegium is
suggested by the expansion of the monograms
as Lares Regienses.
Moneyer: L. Caesius.

110 Denarius *c.* 105 BC

Obv. Bust of Roma, helmeted and holding
spear and shield, l.; to l., ✖; above,
crescent; to r., ROMA.
Rev. Voting scene in the comitium. In
foreground on the *pons* one figure on l.
receives tabella from half-length figure
and second drops tabella into box;
above, tribune's chair with tabella
inscribed P, and P.N͡ERVA. Æ, 3.95 gm. ↓.
Moneyer: P. Licinius Nerva.

111   Denarius *c.* 105 BC

Obv. Within a surrounding torque, head of Roma, helmeted, r.; to l., ROMA; under chin, ✖.

Rev. Warrior, with spear and shield, galloping l.; above, Q; below, T. TORQVA; in ex., EX.S.C. ᴁ, 3.89 gm. ←.

A punning type. The torque is an allusion to an ancestor of the moneyer (L. Manlius Torquatus) who took the torque from a Gaul slain in single combat. The initial, Q, is the first reference to quaestors as moneyers, and the formula EX.SC marks this as a special issue by decree of the senate.

112   Denarius *c.* 105 BC

Obv. Head of Philip V of Macedon in helmet of skin ornamented with goat's horns, r.; to l., ᴭ; under chin, Φ.

Rev. Statue of horseman, with branch over shoulder, r.; beneath horse, a flower.; on statue base, L. PHILLIPVS; below, ✖. ᴁ, 3.90 gm. ↓.

An earlier L. Marcius Philippus had been engaged on a diplomatic mission to Philip V.

113   Denarius *c.* 105 BC

Obv. Head of Roma, helmeted, r.; to l., ᴭ; below, ✖.

Rev. Warrior, with whip and shield, r., fighting warrior, with sword and shield, l.; in ex., T.DEIDI. ᴁ, 3.86 gm. ↓.

The reverse may refer to a T. Didius who, as praetor in Sicily, quelled a slave revolt in 138 BC.

114   Denarius *c.* 105 BC

Obv. Head of Roma, helmeted, r., to l., P.LAECA; above, ROMA; below chin, X.

Rev. Soldier in cuirass standing l., placing hand on head of togate figure standing r.; to r., lictor holding fasces; in ex., PROVOCO. ᴁ, 3.82 gm. ↓.

The *lex de provocatione* giving a citizen outside Rome the right to appeal against a magistrate acting in a military capacity was passed by an earlier Porcius Laeca in 195 BC.

115   Denarius *c.* 100 BC

Obv. Head of Roma, helmeted; r.; to l., SER. to r.; ROMA.

Rev. Sol in facing quadriga rising from the sea; to l. and r., a star; above crescent and X. ᴁ, 4.02 gm. ↘.

The reverse alludes to the victories in the East of Manlius Vulso in 189 BC.
Moneyer: A. Manlius Sergia.

116 Denarius *c.* 100 BC

Obv. Jugate heads of the Dioscuri, laureate, r.;
    above, two stars; to r., ✖ and P P.
Rev. Galley with pilot r.; above, M̂N.FONT̂EI;
    below, C. Æ, 3.95 gm. ↑.
The letters P P on obverse suggest that the
Dioscuri are here represented as the Penates
Publici. This series is an early example of the
use of a sequence letter on the reverse as a
control mark.
Moneyer: Manius Fonteius.

117 Denarius *c.* 100 BC

Obv. Head of Roma, helmeted, l.; to r., S.
Rev. Saturn, holding falx, in quadriga, r.;
    below, ·B· in ex., L.SATURN.
    Æ, 3.86 gm. ←.
An example of a *type parlant*: Saturn is
represented on the reverse of an issue by the
moneyer, L. Saturninus.

118 Denarius *c.* 100 BC

Obv. Head of Pietas, diademed, r.; to l.,
    PIET̂AS; below chin, Ḟ.
Rev. Naked youth running r.; and bearing an
    old man, on his shoulder: to l.
    M.HERENNI. Æ, 3.89 gm. ↑.

An illustration of the story of the brothers
Amphinomus and Anapias of Catana who
carried their parents to safety during an
eruption of Mount Etna.
Moneyer: M. Herennius.

119 Quinarius *c.* 100 BC

Obv. Head of Jupiter, laureate, r.; to l., E.
Rev. Victory, standing r., placing wreath on
    trophy of arms, at foot of which a
    bound captive kneels, l.; to r., C. FVN̂DA;
    in ex., Q. Æ, 1.84 gm. ↖.
The quinarius, long out of issue, was revived
about this date, but now with the types of the
victoriate.
Moneyer: C. Fundanius.

120 Denarius *c.* 95 BC

Obv. Bust of Minerva, with helmet and aegis,
    l.; to r., RVLLI.
Rev. Victory in biga of horses, r.; below, P;
    in ex., P.SERVILLI.M.F. 3.91 gm. →.
P (*Publice*) indicates the public treasury as the
source of the bullion for this special issue.
Moneyer: P. Servillius Rullus.

121 Denarius *c.* 95 BC

Obv. Head of Saturn, laureate, r.; to r., harpa;
around, PISO-CAEPIO, Q; below, trident.
Rev. Two figures seated l. on subsellium; on
each side, a corn-ear; in ex. AD.FRV.EMV.
EX.S.C. Æ, 3.76 gm. ↖.
An issue struck by the quaestors for the
purchase of corn in accordance with a
senatorial decree.
Moneyers: L. Calpurnius Piso and Q. Servilius
Caepio.

122 Denarius *c.* 93 BC

Obv. Head of Apollo laureate, r.; around,
L.POMPON.MOLO.
Rev. Numa Pompilius, holding lituus,
standing r., by altar; youth standing l.,
holding sacrificial goat; in ex., NVMA
POMPIL Æ, 3.92 gm. ↓.
Moneyer: L. Pomponius Molo.

123 Denarius *c.* 92 BC

Obv. Head of Apollo, laureate, r.; to l., star of
ten rays; below, R; to r., X.
Rev. The Dioscuri standing l. by horses
drinking from the fountain of Joturna;
in ex. A. ALBINVS S. F. Æ, 3.89 gm. ↙.
In the battle of Lake Regillus in 497 BC the
Dioscuri aided the Romans against the Latins,
and were seen on the evening of the battle
watering their horses at the fountain of Joturna
in the Forum.
Moneyer: A. Postumius Albinus.

4 The Social War and its Aftermath 91–79 BC

Rome's continued refusal to extend the privileges of citizenship to her allies in Italy led to their formation into the so-called Marsic Confederation, and to open revolt. The coinage issued by the Confederation consists, with the exception of a unique aureus, of silver denarii. These fall essentially into two groups: one with inscriptions in Latin, and another with inscriptions in Oscan. The capital of the Confederation was at Corfinium, but the mint, or mints, of the coinage remain uncertain. A number of issues closely copy the types of the Roman denarii of the preceding years, but a less numerous class present more original propagandistic types.

The exigencies of the war produced, on the Roman side, some of the most prolific denarius issues of the Republican series. The practice of placing control marks on the dies in the form of letters, numerals, or symbols which had appeared earlier in a number of issues reached its most elaborate form on a number of the immense issues of this period. In the bronze coinage the effective decline of weight to a semuncial standard was officially recognised by the *lex Papiria semunciaria* in 89 BC which is noted in the formula used on at least one bronze issue (No. 133).

The first phases of the resumed struggle between the senatorial and democratic parties at Rome on the conclusion of the Social War, Sulla's successful march on Rome in 88 BC, and the subsequent Marian terror following Sulla's departure for the Mithridatic campaign in 87 BC made scarcely any impact on coin typology. Sulla's return to Italy and the Marian defeat at the Colline Gate in 82 BC, however, was accompanied by the first 'imperatorial' coinage, including the first substantial coinage in gold since the late third century. This coinage bearing Sulla's name, though it has, traditionally, been regarded as a provincial issue struck in Greece, may possibly have continued to be issued after his return to Italy. Other provincial coinages in the Sullan period include issues in Gaul by Valerius Flaccus in his capacity as imperator, and for C. Annius Luscus, proconsul in Spain, for the campaign against Sertorius, the Marian governor.

124 Denarius 91–88 BC

Obv. Head of Italia, laureate, l.; to r., ITALIA.
Rev. Youth kneeling at foot of standard, and holding pig, at which eight soldiers, four on either side, point sword; in ex., P. Æ, 3.86 gm. ↓.
For 'oath-scene' cf. Nos. 34, 82, 127.

125 Denarius 91–88 BC

Obv. Head of youthful Bacchus, ivy-wreathed, r., all within laurel-wreath.
Rev. Bull r., trampling on she-wolf; below, VIƝƎTⱵⱭ; above Ɲ. Æ, 4.00 gm. ↙.
On the reverse the bull and she-wolf symbolise talia and Rome respectively. The Oscan inscription = Vitelliu = Italia.

126 Denarius 90–88 BC

Obv. Head of Italia, helmeted, r.; below, **ITALIA**.

Rev. The Dioscuri riding in opposite directions; in ex., ⊃·Ⅰⵑⵕⵕⵕ·⊃. Æ, 3.95 gm. ↑.

The reverse is a copy of No. 91. The Oscan inscription = C. Paapi C., the name of the Marsic general C. Papius C. F. Mutilus.

127 Denarius 91–88 BC

Obv. Head of Italia, helmeted, r.; to l., ẋ and ꔮ.

Rev. Youth kneeling and holding pig between four soldiers, two on either side, who touch pig with sword; in ex., ·⊃·ꓲⵑⵕⵕⵕ·⊃. Æ, 3.95 gm. ↓.

The types of both obverse and reverse copy those of the denarius of Ti Veturius, No. 82.

128 Denarius 91–88 BC

Obv. Head of Italia, laureate, l.; below chin, X; TO R., ꔮ.

Rev. Soldier standing facing, head r.; holding spear and sword; to r., recumbent bull; to l., ꔮ·ⵍⵎⵛꓘⵏ·Ⅰꔮ; in ex., ꞵ. Æ, 4.02 gm. →.

The Oscan inscription = Ni Luvki Mr, the name of another Marsic general.

129 Denarius 91–88 BC

Obv. Bust of Italia, in helmet and aegis, r., crowned by Victory.

Rev. Soldier, holding spear, standing r., clasping hands with figure, holding globe, standing l., by prow of ship; in ex., ꒐. Æ, 4.22 gm. ↓.

The figure with globe on the reverse probably represents Mithradates who had promised help to the Marsic confederacy.

130 Denarius 90–89 BC

Obv. Head of Apollo, laureate, r.; to l., FRVGI; to r., cap of Dioscuri.

Rev. Horseman galloping l., carrying torch; below, L. PISO L. F.; above, thunderbolt. Æ, 3.97 gm. ←.

This war coinage of Rome is one of the most prolific issues of a single moneyer (L. Piso Frugi), and is remarkable for the great variety of die control marks.

131 Denarius 89–88 BC

Obv. Head of Pan, goat-eared, r.; below,
PANSA.

Rev. Head of Silenus, ivy-wreathed, r.;
below. C·VĪBIVS·C·F. Æ, 3.77 gm. ↓.

Another prolific issue in Rome's Social war
coinage, and another example of a *type parlant*.
Moneyer: C. Vibius Pansa.

132 Sestertius 89 BC

Obv. Head of Apollo, laureate, r.; to l., PISO.

Rev. Horse galloping r.; above, E.L.P.; below,
FRVGI. Æ, 0.95 gm. ↓.

For E.L.P. = *ex lege Papiria* see No. 133.
Moneyer: L. Piso Frugi.

133 Triens 89 BC

Obv. Head of Minerva helmeted laureate;
above, • • • •.

Rev. Prow r.; below, • • • •; above, L.P.D.A.P.
Æ, 4.41 gm. ←.

The formula on the reverse is expanded as *lege
Papiria de aere publico*. The *lex Papiria* of early
89 BC gave recognition to the reduction of the
bronze unit to the semuncial standard.

134 Denarius *c*. 88 BC

Obv. Head of Tatius r.; to l., SABIN; to r., Ā .

Rev. Two soldiers r. and l., each carrying off
a Sabine woman; in ex., L.TITVRI. Æ,
4.02 gm. ↖.

The types of the Sabine king, Tatius, and the
story of the rape of the Sabine women are apt
for a moneyer with the cognomen Sabinus.

135 As *c*. 86 BC

Obv. Janiform heads of Hercules and
Mercury; to l., club; to r., caduceus.

Rev. Distyle temple containing altar; to l.,
DOSSE; to r., prow; in ex., L.RVBRI.
Æ, 9.72 gm. ↗.

A departure from the traditional types of this
denomination.
Moneyer: L. Rubrius Dossena.

136 Denarius *c*. 86 BC

Obv. Heads of Numa Pompilius and Ancus
Martius, diademed, jugate, r.

Rev. Two horses, on nearer of which a rider
with whip and conical cap, galloping r.;
below, rudder; in ex., C.CENSO.
Æ, 4.04 gm. ↙.

The moneyer, C. Marcius Censorinus, was a
supporter of Marius and Cinna. The family
claimed descent from the early kings, Numa
and Ancus Martius.

137 Denarius *c.* 85 BC

Obv. Head of Ceres, with corn-wreath, r.; to
l., AED.PL.
Rev. M. Fannius and L. Critonius, togate,
seated r.; l., PA; to r., corn-ear; in ex.,
M.FAN L.CRĪT. Ǎ, 4.06 gm. ↑.
A special issue made by Fannius and Critanius
as *aediles plebei* from bullion from the public
treasury, *publico argento*.

138 Denarius *c.* 84 BC

Obv. Head of Veiovis, laureate, r.; to l., MN̂.
FONTEI; below, thunderbolt; below
chin, C.F.
Rev. Infant Genius, seated on goat, r., caps of
the Dioscuri on either side; in ex.,
thyrsus with fillet; all within laurel-
wreath. Ǎ, 4.34 gm. ↑.
A goat bearing a winged Genius stood near the
statue of Veiovis in his temple in Rome.
Moneyer: Manius Fonteius.

139 Denarius *c.* 84 BC

Obv. As No. 138, but on l., EX A.P.
Rev. As No. 138. Ǎ, 3.97 gm. ↗.
Another special issue from the public treasury,
ex argento publico.

140 Denarius *c.* 83 BC

Obv. Female head, turreted, r.; to l., AED.CVR,
and deformed foot.
Rev. Curule chair inscribed P.FOVRIVS; in ex.,
CRASSIPES. Ǎ, 4.17 gm. ←.
The deformed foot symbol on the obverse is a
pun on the moneyer's cognomen Crassipes. A
special issue by a curule aedile.

141 Aureus *c.* 82 BC

Obv. Head of Roma, helmeted, r.; on r.,
L.MANLI; on l., PRO.Q.
Rev. Sulla in triumphal quadriga, r.; above
Victory with wreath.; in ex., L.SVLLA IM.
Ǎ, 10.97 gm. ↑.
Moneyer: L. Manlius.

142 Aureus *c.* 82 BC

Obv. Head of Venus, r.; to r., Cupid standing
l., holding palm-branch; below,
L.SVLLA.
Rev. Jug and lituus between two trophies;
above, IMPER; below, ITERVM.
Ǎ, 10.73 gm. ↑.

143 Aureus *c.* 81 BC

Obv. Bust of Roma, helmeted, draped, r.; to
l., A.MANLI; to r.; A.F.Q.
Rev. Equestrian statue of Sulla, r. hand raised,
to l.; in ex., L.SVLL FE [LI DIC].
N, 10.87 gm. ↙.
Moneyer: A. Manlius.

144 Denarius *c.* 82 BC

Obv. Head of Apollo, laureate, r.
Rev. The satyr, Marsyas, with wine skin on
shoulder, walking l.; to r., draped figure
on column; to l., L.CENSOR. AR, 4.39 gm. →.
The obverse and reverse types taken together
may refer to the musical contest between
Apollo and Marsyas.
Moneyer: L. Censorinus.

145 Denarius *c.* 82 BC

Obv. Bust of Mercury with winged *petasus*,
r.; to l; caduceus and Ᵽ.
Rev. Ulysses with staff in l. hand, walking r.,
and extending r. hand to dog, Argus; to
l., C.MAMIL, to r., LIMETAN. AR, 3.87 gm. ←.
The Mamilian family claimed descent from
Ulysses, in turn descended from Mercury.
Moneyer: C. Mamilius Limetanus.

146 Denarius *c.* 81 BC

Obv. Head of Jupiter, laureate, r.; to l., D.
Rev. Europa, holding veil over head, seated
on bull, l.; on r., winged thunderbolt;
below, vine-leaf; in ex., L·VOL·L·F·STRAB.
AR, 3.86 gm. ↓.
Moneyer: L. Volteius Strabo.

147 Denarius *c.* 79 BC

Obv. Head of Hispania, veiled, r.; to l.
HISPAN.
Rev. Togate figure, standing l., raising r.
hand over legionary eagle; on r.; fasces
with axe; in field and ex., A.POST.
A.F.S.N. ALBIN. AR, 3.96 gm. →.
Moneyer: A. Postumius Albinus.

148 Denarius *c.* 82 BC

Obv. Bust of Victory, draped and winged, r.;
on r., branch.
Rev. Legionary eagle between two standards,
the left inscribed H, the right P; on l., C.
VAL.FLA [C. Valerius Flaccus]; on r.;
IMPERAT; below EX S.C. AR, 3.95 gm. ↓.
Gallic mintage.

149 Denarius *c.* 81 BC

Obv. Bust of Anna Perenna, diademed,
       draped, r.; to l., caduceus; to r., scales;
       around, C.ANNI. T.F. T.N. PRO.COS. EX S.C.
Rev. Victory in quadriga, r.; above, Q;
       [Quaestor;] ex., L.FABI.L·F. HISP.
       Æ, 3.94 gm. ↓.
Struck by Fabius, quaestor of the proconsul in
Spain, C. Annius Luscus. Perhaps struck in
north Italy.

5 Pompey and Caesar 78-44 BC

The coinage of this period continued to be basically one of silver denarii, but later, particularly after Caesar's return to Italy in 49 BC there were frequent and extensive issues of gold aurei, and the occasional issue of bronze once again. The typology of the coins was still largely concerned with allusions to the history of the moneyers' families, but a growing tendency to refer to men and events of comparatively recent history paved the way for the portraying and honouring of a living person at the end of this period with the issue of a portrait series for Caesar in early 44 BC.

The bulk of the coinage continued to be produced by the mint of Rome, but political rivalry and the ensuing civil war brought a considerable increase in 'imperatorial' and military issues. Coinage was struck for Caesar as proconsul in Gaul from 59 BC, and the Pompeians, after the withdrawal from Italy in 49 BC, produced issues in Sicily, Greece, Spain and Africa.

150 Denarius *c*. 78 BC

Obv. Head of Roma, helmeted, r.; to l., ROMA. above, F.
Rev. Hercules standing l., strangling the Nemean lion; at feet, club; to l., bow and arrows in case; or r., C.POBLICI.Q.F; above, K. Æ, 3.80 gm. →.
Moneyer: C. Poblicius.

151 Denarius *c*. 78 BC

Obv. Head of Juno Sospita, with goat-skin head-dress, r.; to l., cray-fish.
Rev. Gryphon r.; below, sepia; in ex., L.PAPI. Æ, 3.39 gm. ↘.
The moneyer's family presumably had a connection with Lanuvium where Juno Caprotina was worshipped.
Moneyer: L. Papius.

152 Denarius *c*. 78 BC

Obv. Head of Jupiter, laureate, r.
Rev. Tetrastyle temple of Jupiter Capitolinus, with closed doors and thunderbolt ornament in pediment; in ex., M.VOLTEI.M.F. Æ, 3.82 gm. ↓.
The chief annual agonistic festivals are referred to by the reverses of Nos 152–6. The reference here is to the *ludi Romani*.
Moneyer: M. Volteius.

153   Denarius *c.* 78 BC

Obv. Head of Hercules, with lion skin head-
       dress, r.
Rev. The Erymanthian boar r.; in ex.
       M.VOLTEI.M.F. Æ, 3.93 gm. ↘.
Reference to the *ludi Plebeii.*

154   Denarius *c.* 78 BC

Obv. Head of Bacchus, ivy-wreathed, r.
Rev. Ceres, holding torch in either hand, in
       chariot drawn by two serpents, r.; to l.,
       plectrum; in ex., M.VOLTEI.M.F.
       Æ, 3.86 gm. ↘.
Reference to the *ludi Cereales.*

155   Denarius *c.* 78 BC

Obv. Head of Attis, helmeted, draped, r.; to
       l., owl.
Rev. Cybele, holding patera in r. hand, in
       chariot drawn by two lions, r.; above
       KA; in ex., M.VOLTEI.M.F.
       Æ, 3.89 gm. ↗.
Reference to the *ludi Megalenses.*

156   Denarius *c.* 78 BC

Obv. Head of Apollo, laureate, r.
Rev. Tripod with serpent entwined round
       centre leg; to l., SC.; to r., D.T.; in ex.
       M.VOLTEI.M.F. Æ, 3.84 gm. ↙.
Reference to the *ludi Apollinares.* The formula,
S.C.D.T. (*Senatus consulto de thesauro*), suggests
that this special issue was financed from the
treasury by decree.

157   Denarius *c.* 75 BC

Obv. Head of Liber, ivy-wreathed, r., with
       thyrsus over l. shoulder.
Rev. Head of Libera, crowned with vine and
       grapes, l; L.CASSI.Q.F. Æ, 4.02 gm. ←.
An ancestor of the moneyer, Spurius Cassius,
dedicated a temple at the foot of the Aventine
to these deities as well as to Ceres in 493 BC.

158   Denarius *c.* 75 BC

Obv. Bust of Libertas, draped and diademed,
       r.; to l., *pileus* and S.C.; to r., MENSOR.
Rev. Roma in biga of horses r., assists togate
       figure into chariot; below, XXII; in ex.,
       L.FARSVLEI. Æ, 3.92 gm. ↓.
Moneyer: L. Farsuleius Mensor.

159 Denarius. *c.* 75 BC

Obv. Head of Hercules r.; to l., Q.S.C.
Rev. Genius of the Roman people, holding cornucopiae and sceptre and crowned by Victory, standing facing by curule chair; to l., P.LENT.P.F; to r., L.N. Æ, 4.13 gm. ←.
A special issue by a quaestor, P. Cornelius Lentulus.

160 Denarius *c.* 75 BC

Obv. Head of Medusa, winged and entwined with serpents. l.; to r., SABVLA.
Rev. Bellerophon mounted on Pegasus, and hurling spear, r.; to l., XIII; below, L.COSSVTI.C.F. Æ, 3.71 gm. →.
Moneyer: L. Cossutius Sabula.

161 Denarius *c.* 75 BC

Obv. Bust of Cupid, winged, and with bow and quiver on back, r.; to l., MAXSUMUS.
Rev. Distyle temple containing standing figures of Jupiter and Libertas; in tympanum, thunderbolt and pileus; to l., VII; in ex., C.EGNATIUS.CN.F; to r., [CN.N]. Æ, 3.65 gm. ↙.
Moneyer: C. Egnatius Maxsumus.

162 Denarius *c.* 70 BC

Obv. Bust of Amphitrite, seen from back, r.; to l., tortoise; to r., B and countermark SO.
Rev. Neptune, hurling trident, in sea-chariot drawn by two hippocamps, r.; above, A.; below, Q.CREPER.M.[F]ROCVS. Æ, 3.89 gm. ↓.
Moneyer: Q. Crepereius Rocus.

163 Denarius *c.* 70 BC

Obv. Bust of Virtus, helmeted, draped, r.; to l., III VIR; to r., VIRTUS.
Rev. The consul, Manius Aquillius, standing l.; head r., holding shield and raising figure of Sicilia, kneeling l.; to r., MN AQVIL; to l., MN. F.MN; in ex., SICIL. Æ, 3.91 gm. ↘, serrate.
An ancestor of the moneyer (Manius Aquillius) conducted a successful campaign against a revolt of slaves in Sicily in 101 BC.

164 Denarius *c.* 70 BC

Obv. Bust of Juno Moneta, diademed, draped, r.; to l.; below chin, SC.
Rev. Naked athlete, holding palm-branch and caestus, running r.; to l., L.PLAETORI; to r., L.F.Q.S.C. Æ, 3.85 gm. ↘ .

The formula, Q.S.C. (*quaestor, senatus consulto*) marks this as a special issue by L. Plaetorius.

165 Denarius 70 BC

Obv. Jugate heads r., of Honos, laureate, and Virtus, helemeted; to l., HO; to r., VIRT; below KALENI.
Rev. Italia standing r. holding cornucopiae and clasping hands with Roma standing, helmeted, holding spear and placing foot on globe; to l., ITAL; to r., RO; in ex., CORDI. Æ, 3.90 gm. ↘ , serrate.

Perhaps a somewhat tardy allusion to the end of the Social War.
Moneyers: Kalenus and Cordus.

166 Denarius *c.* 70 BC

Obv. Head of Tatius, bearded, r.; to l., SABINVS; to r., S.C; below chin, Ⱶ.
Rev. Togate figure, holding sceptre, in biga, l.; to r., corn-ear; above, IVDEX; in ex., T.VETTIVS. Æ, 4.02 gm. ↗ , serrate.

The obverse is a punning type similar to that of No. 134. The charioteer on the reverse, labelled *Iudex*, probably represents the interrex, Spurius Vettius, an ancestor, who supported the election of king Numa.
Moneyer: T. Vettius Sabinus.

167 Denarius *c.* 68 BC

Obv. Head of Fortuna, l.; to r., sword.
Rev. Pediment of temple containing snake-footed giant holding club in l. hand; on base of pediment, M.PLAETOR below, CEST.S.C. Æ, 3.87 gm. ↙ .

The moneyer, M. Plaetorius Cestianus, is identified on one of his types as a curule aedile, who held office about 68 BC. The obverse is probably Fortuna and the reverse shows part of her famous temple at Praeneste.

168 Denarius *c.* 68 BC

Obv. As No. 167 but head r.; to l., scales.
Rev. Half-length figure of Sors, draped, facing; below, tablet inscribed SORS; around, M.PLAETORI CEST.S.C. Æ, 3.96 gm. ↙ .

The *Sortes Praenestinae* were associated with the cult of Fortuna.

169 Denarius *c.* 65 BC

Obv. Head of Apollo, bound with fillet, r.; to
l., ram's head.
Rev. Naked horseman r.; below, C PISO L.F.
FRV and Ǝ. Æ, 4.06 gm. ↓.
The types are almost identical with those used
by the moneyer's father (see No. 130).
Moneyer: C. Piso Frugi.

170 Denarius *c.* 65 BC

Obv. Head of Roma, laureate, r.
Rev. Equestrian statue, bearing trophy, r.;
around, M.LEPIDVS.AN XV. PR. H.O.C.S.
Æ, 4.11 gm. ↓.
The statue is that said to have been erected in
honour of the moneyer's ancestor, M.
Aemilius Lepidus, consul in 187 BC, who at the
age of fifteen slew an enemy and saved a citizen
as the reverse inscription, *annorum quindecim
progressus hostem occidit, civem servavit* records.

171 Denarius *c.* 65 BC

Obv. Head of Alexandria, turreted, r.
Rev. Togate figure, standing r., and placing
wreath on head of youth in Greek dress,
standing front; in ex. and around,
M.LEPIDVS TVTOR REG. S.C. PONT MAX. Æ,
3.99 gm. ↑.

The types refer to the same Lepidus as on No.
170. He was one of the Roman administrators
appointed during the minority of Ptolemy V
of Egypt, *c.* 200 BC.

172 Denarius *c.* 65 BC

Obv. Head of Vestal virgin, Aemilia, laureate,
veiled, r.; to l., wreath; to r., simpulum.
Rev. The Basilica Aemilia with circular
shields attached to the columns.;
around, M LEPIDVS AIMILIA REF SC.
Æ, 3.94 gm. ↘.
The moneyer's father, as consul in 78 BC,
restored this temple.

173 Denarius *c.* 65 BC

Obv. Head of Apollo, diademed, r.; around,
Q. POMPONIVS MVSA.
Rev. Hercules, wearing lion-skin, standing r.,
playing lyre; at foot, right, club; to r.,
HERCULES; to l., MVSARVM.
Æ, 3.76 gm. →.
This and the following coins (Nos 174–82)
with representations of Hercules as leader of
the muses, and the nine muses themselves, are
types punning on the name of the moneyer,
Musa.
Moneyer: Q. Pomponius Musa.

174 Denarius *c.* 65 BC

Obv. Head of Apollo, laureate, r.; to l., lyre-
key.
Rev. Calliope, standing r., playing lyre set on
pedestal; to l., POMPONI; to r., MVSA.
Æ, 3.90 gm. ↘.
Calliope, the muse of epic poetry.

175 Denarius *c.* 65 BC

Obv. As No. 174, but to l., scroll tied with
cord.
Rev. As No. 174, but Clio, standing l.,
holding scroll in r. hand and resting l.
elbow on pedestal. Æ, 3.83 gm. ↗.
Clio, the muse of history.

176 Denarius *c.* 65 BC

Obv. As No. 174, but to l., flower.
Rev. As No. 174, but Erato, standing r;
striking lyre with plectrum.
Æ, 4.02 gm. ↘.
Erato, the muse of love poetry.

177 Denarius *c.* 65 BC

Obv. As No. 174, but to l.; two pipes crossed.
Rev. As No. 174, but Euterpe r., resting l.
elbow on pedestal, and holding two
pipes. Æ, 4.01 gm. ↓.
Euterpe, the muse of lyric poetry.

178 Denarius *c.* 65 BC

Obv. As No. 174, but to l.; sceptre.
Rev. As No. 174, but Melpomene, standing
front, head r., holding club and mask.
Æ, 3.78 gm. ↘.
Melpomene, the muse of tragedy.

179 Denarius *c.* 65 BC

Obv. As No. 174, but to l., wreath with fillet.
Rev. As No. 174, but Polymnia, standing
facing. Æ, 3.81 gm. ↓.
Polymnia, the muse of rhetoric.

180 Denarius *c.* 65 BC

Obv. As No. 174, but to l., flower.
Rev. Terpsichore, standing r., holding lyre in l. hand and plectrum in r.
Æ, 3.95 gm. ↙.
Terpsichore, the muse of dance.

181 Denarius *c.* 65 BC

Obv. As No. 174, but to l., sandal.
Rev. As No. 174, but Thalia, standing l., l. elbow on pedestal and mask in right hand. Æ, 3.73 gm. ↗.
Thalia, the muse of comedy.

182 Denarius *c.* 65 BC

Obv. As No. 174, but to l., star.
Rev. As No. 174, but Urania, standing r., touching, with wand in r. hand, globe set on tripod. Æ, 3.93 gm. ↙.
Urania, the muse of astronomy.

183 Denarius *c.* 65 BC

Obv. Head of Sibyl, ivy-wreathed, r.; below, SIBVLLA; all within a laurel-wreath.
Rev. Tripod, surmounted by amphora between two stars; to l., L.TORQUAT; to r., III.VIR; all within a torque.
Æ, 3.89 gm. ↘.

The enclosing torque is again a pun on the moneyer's name. L. Torquatus. The types allude to the consultation of the Sibylline books and the celebration of the games of Apollo, duties of the college *sacris faciundis*.

184 Denarius *c.* 65 BC

Obv. Head of Juno Sospita, wearing goat-skin head-dress, r.; to l., conical cap with strings.
Rev. Female figure, draped, standing r., feeding serpent, head raised; to l., club; in ex., FABATI. Æ, 3.92 gm. ↘, serrate.
The reverse illustrates one of the ceremonies of the festival of Juno Sospita at Lanuvium.
Moneyer: L. Roscius Fabatius.

185 Denarius *c.* 60 BC

Obv. Head of Saturn r., to l., harpa, baetyl and S.C.; to r. SVFENAS.
Rev. Roma, holding spear and sword, seated l. on pile of arms, and crowned by Victory standing l., holding palm-branch; in ex. and around, SEX,NONI PR.L.V.P.F. Æ, 4.03 gm. ↘.
The formula PR.L.V.P.F. (*praetor ludos Victoriae primus fecit*) alludes to the Victory games inaugurated by Sextus Nonnius, praetor in 81 BC, to celebrate Sulla's victory at the Colline Gate.
Moneyer: Sufenas.

186 Denarius *c.* 60 BC

Obv. Bust of Diana, draped, diademed, r.; to
l., lituus; above, crescent; to r., FAVSTVS.

Rev. Sulla seated l.; before him Bocchus
holding olive-branch kneeling r.;
behind, Jugurtha, hands bound, kneeling l.; to r., FELIX. Æ, 3.87 gm. ↓.

The reverse of this issue by the son of the
dictator, commemorates Sulla's success, the
submission in 100 BC of Bocchus, king of
Mauretania, and his surrender of Jugurtha,
king of Numidia.

Moneyer: Faustus Sulla.

187 Denarius *c.* 60 BC

Obv. Bust of young Hercules, draped in lion-
skin, r.; to l., FELIX.

Rev. Diana, crescent above head, holding
lituus, in biga, r.; above, two stars;
below, star and FAVSTVS. Æ, 3.89 gm. ↓.

The obverse portrait is sometimes identified as
that of Jugurtha.

188 Denarius *c.* 60 BC

Obv. Bust of Venus, laureate, diademed,
draped, r.; to l., C.CONSIDI.NONIANI; to r.,
S.C.

Rev. Temple, surrounded by rampart with
gateway at centre and tower at each
side, on top of mountain; above gate.
ERVC. Æ, 3.95 gm. →.

The cult of Venus of Eryx in Sicily was
brought to Rome in the late third century and
in 181 BC a temple was built outside the Porta
Collatina.

Moneyer: C. Considius Nonianus.

189 Aureus *c.* 61 BC

Obv. Head of Africa, in elephant-skin, r.; to
l., jug and MAGNUS; to r., lituus; all
within laurel-wreath.

Rev. Pompey, holding laurel-wreath, in
triumphal quadriga r.; on nearest horse,
a youth; above, Victory with wreath; in
ex., PRO.COS. Ν, 8.93 gm. ↙.

The triumph depicted is probably that
accorded to Pompey after his successes against
the pirates and Mithradates.

190 Denarius *c.* 55 BC

Obv. Head of Vesta, diademed, veiled, r.; to
l., Q.CASSIVS; to r., VEST.

Rev. Domed, circular temple of Vesta,
surmounted by figure holding sceptre
and patera; to l., urn; to r., tablet
inscribed AC. Æ, 3.97 gm. →.

The types including the voting urn and tablet
with inscription A C (*absolvo : condemno*) allude
to a trial of the Vestal virgins in 113 BC presided

over by L. Cassius Longinus Ravilla.
Moneyer: Q. Cassius.

191 Denarius *c.* 60 BC

Obv. Head of Concordia, diademed, veiled r.;
around, P.FONTEIVS. CAPITO. III.VIR.
CONCORDIA.

Rev. Two-storied building with columns; in
field and ex., T.DIDI.IMP.VIL.PVB.
Æ, 3.96 gm. ↙.

The reverse suggests that T. Didius, given a
triumph and the title of imperator in 93 BC,
restored the Villa Publica in the Campus
Martius.

Moneyer: P. Fonteius Capito.

192 Denarius *c.* 60 BC

Obv. Head of Libertas, r.; to l., LIBERTAS.

Rev. The consul L. Junius Brutus walking l.,
between two lictors, and preceded by an
accensus, in ex., BRVTVS. Æ, 4.11 gm. ↗.

M. Junius Brutus, later one of the assassins of
Caesar, recalls on the reverse his ancestor who,
after the expulsion of the kings in 509 BC
became consul.

193 Denarius *c.* 60 BC

Obv. Head of Lucius Junius Brutus, r.; to l.,
BRUTUS.

Rev. Head of Caius Servilius Ahala, r.; to l.,
AHALA. Æ, 4.07 gm. ←.

Portraits of Brutus's famous ancestors, the
consul Brutus and Servilius Ahala who
executed Spurius Maelius for plotting against
the state.

194 Denarius *c.* 60 BC

Obv. Head of the consul, Pompeius Rufus, r.;
to l., RVFUS.COS; to r., Q.POM.RVFI.

Rev. Head of Sulla, r.; to r., SVLLA COS.
Æ, 4.02 gm. ↙.

Portraits of the moneyer's grandfathers, Rufus
and Sulla, who were consuls in 88 BC.

Moneyer: Q. Pompeius Rufus.

195 Denarius 57 BC

Obv. King Aretas, kneeling r., holding olive-
branch in r. hand, and bridle of camel in
l.; above, M.SCAVR AED CVR; to l. and r.,
EX S.C.; in ex., REX ARETAS.

Rev. Jupiter hurling thunderbolt, in quadriga
r.; below horses, scorpion; above
P.HYPSAEVS AED CVR; below, C HYPSAE
COS PREIVER; to r. CAPTV. Æ, 4.08 gm. ↘.

Scaurus and Hypsaeus were curule aediles in 57
BC. Scaurus, as governor of Syria in 64 BC,
compelled the submission to Pompey of the
Nabataean king, Aretas. The reverse commemorates the capture of Privernum by the
consul Hypsaeus in 329 BC.

196   Denarius *c.* 55 BC

Obv. Head of Concordia, diademed, veiled, r.; to l., PAVLLVS. LEPIDVS; to r., CON-CORDIA.

Rev. Trophy; to r., togate figure, standing l.; to l., figure with bound hands, accompanied by two youths, standing l.; above, TER; in ex., PAVLLVS. Æ, 3.87 gm. ↓.

The reverse alludes to the defeat of Perseus of Macedon by L. Aemilius Paullus in 168 BC.

197   Denarius 55 BC

Obv. Head of Bonus Eventus, diademed, r.; to l., LIBO; to r., BON.EVENT.

Rev. Puteal, or well-head, ornamented with festoon between two lyres with a hammer below; above, PUTEAL; below, SCRIBON. Æ, 4.11 gm. ↘.

The puteal erected in the Forum by a Scribonius marked a spot struck by lightning and hence was considered sacred.
Moneyer: L. Scribonius Libo.

198   Denarius *c.* 55 BC

Obv. Head of Ancus Marcius, diademed, r.; to l., lituus.

Rev. Equestrian statue r., on arcade of five arches containing AQVA·MA͡R; to l., PHILIPPVS. Æ, 4.02 gm. ↓.

Ancus Marcius, the legendary ancestor of this moneyer's family is credited with first bringing water to Rome by aqueduct. Q. Marcius Rex who built the Aqua Marcia in 144 BC was honoured by an equestrian statue on the aqueduct.

199   Denarius *c.* 54 BC

Obv. Bust of Venus, laureate, diademed, draped, r.; to l., sceptre and s.c.

Rev. Three trophies; to l., jug; to r., lituus. in ex ⚒. Æ, 4.10 gm. →.

An issue by Faustus Cornelius Sulla, as quaestor, in honour of his father-in-law, Pompey. The types allude to the consecration by Pompey of the temple of Venus Victrix, and to his three triumphs.

200   Denarius *c.* 54 BC

Obv. Head of Hercules in lion skin, r.; to l., s.c. and ⚒.

Rev. Globe surrounded by four wreaths of which the upper is jewelled; to l., aplustre; to r., corn-ear. Æ, 3.85 gm. ↘.

The three wreaths represent the triumphs accorded to Pompey and the jewelled wreath the golden chaplet conferred on him in 63 BC.

201 Denarius *c.* 55 BC

Obv. Head of Quirinus, laureate, r.; to l., QVIRINVS; to r., C.MEMMI.C.F.
Rev. Ceres, holding corn-ears and torch, seated r.; at foot, serpent; around, MEMMIVS.AED.CVR. CERIALIA.PREIMVS.FECIT. Æ, 3.97 gm. ↓.

The reverse refers to the institution of the *ludi Cereales* at Rome by an earlier Memmius.

202 Denarius *c.* 55 BC

Obv. Bust of Venus, laureate, draped, r.; to l., S.C.
Rev. Warrior, holding spear in l. hand and horse by bridle in r., standing r.; around, P.CRASSUS.M.F.. Æ, 4.30 gm. →.

The types may refer to a special issue by senatorial decree for the Gallic cavalry raised by Crassus, a legate of Caesar.

203 Denarius 53 BC

Obv. Bust of Roma, helmeted, bare, r., with spear over l. shoulder; to r., MESSAL.F.
Rev. Curule chair between letters s c; below, sceptre and diadem; above, PATRE.COS. Æ, 4.20 gm. ↙.

The explicit reference to the consulship of the moneyer's father fixes the date of this issue. Moneyer: M. Valerius Messala.

204 Denarius *c.* 50 BC

Obv. Head of Apollo, laureate, r.; to l., SER; to r., SVLP.
Rev. Naval trophy, to l., draped figure wearing petasus; to r., nude figure, hands bound, wearing *petasus*. Æ, 4.00 gm. ↘.

An issue, possibly by an ancestor of the emperor Galba, AD 68–9, alluding to some naval victory of an earlier Sulpicius Galba.

205 Denarius *c.* 50 BC

Obv. Head r.; to l., vexillum inscribed HIS; to r., boar, and C.COEL.CALDVS; below head, COS.
Rev. Seated figure on lectisternium; trophy at each end; on front, L.CALDVS/VII.VIR.EPVL; on l., C.CALDVS; on r., IMP.A.X; below CALDVS. III.VIR. Æ, 4.15 gm. ↓.

The obverse honours the moneyer's grandfather who gained military successes in Spain, his father, a septemvir of the *epulo Iovis*, and his uncle, imperator, augur and decemvir. Moneyer: C. Coelius Caldus.

206 Denarius *c.* 50 BC

Obv. Head of M. Claudius Marcellinus, r.; to
    l., trisikelis to r., MARCELLINVS.
Rev. Tetrastyle temple in which togate figure
    places a trophy; to r., MARCELLVS; to r.,
    COS.QVINC. Æ, 3.96 gm. ↖.

The coin records notable events in the career of
Marcellus, five times consul; the trisikelis refers
to the capture of Syracuse in 212 BC, the reverse
to the dedication of the spoil captured from the
Gallic chief. Britomartus in 222 BC.
Moneyer: P. Cornelius Lentulus Marcellinus.

207 Denarius *c.* 49 BC

Obv. Elephant r., trampling on dragon; in
    ex., CAESAR.
Rev. Emblems of the pontificate.
    Æ, 4.08 gm. ↖.

Struck for Caesar, possibly in Cisalpine Gaul.
The obverse symbolises Caesar's recent
victories over the Gauls.

208 Denarius *c.* 49 BC

Obv. Head of Apollo, diademed, r.; below,
    star; around, Q.SICINIVS III.VIR.
Rev. Lion-skin draped on club; on l., arrow;
    on r., bow; around, C.COPONIVS.PR.S.C.
    Æ, 4.07 gm. ↘.

One of the coinages struck by Q. Sicinius for
Pompey in the East and specifically for the
praetor Coponius who commanded part of the
Rhodian fleet.

209 Denarius *c.* 49 BC

Obv. Triskelis with facing winged head of
    Medusa at centre; in each angle, corn-
    ear.
Rev. Jupiter, standing r., holding thunderbolt
    and eagle; to l., LENT MAR; to r., COS and
    pruning-hook. Æ, 4.12 gm. ↙.

Coinage for L. Cornelius Lentulus and C.
Claudius Marcellus, the consuls of 49 BC who
accompanied Pompey when he left Italy. The
obverse suggests mintage in Sicily.

210 Denarius *c.* 49 BC

Obv. Head of Jupiter, r.
Rev. Cult statue of Ephesian Artemis;
    around, L. LENTVLVS MAR.COS.
    Æ, 4.19 gm. ↖.

Another issue for the consuls Lentulus and
Marcellus struck, the reverse suggests, at
Ephesus.

211 Denarius *c.* 49 BC

Obv. Head of Numa Pompilius, r., with
diadem inscribed NVMA; to l.,
CN.PISO.PRO.Q.
Rev. Prow r.; above, MAGN; below, PRO.COS.
Æ, 3.97 gm. ↓.
A coinage issued by the proquaestor Cn.
Calpurnius Piso for the legions in Spain where
Pompey had proconsular rule.

212 Denarius *c.* 49 BC

Obv. Bust of Jupiter, diademed, r.; to l.,
VARRO. PRO. Q.
Rev. Upright sceptre between dolphin and
eagle, in ex., MAG.PRO. COS.
Æ, 3.90 gm. ↗.
Another coinage issued for the Pompeian party
in Spain by Terentius Varro.

213 Denarius *c.* 49 BC

Obv. Head of a Gaul r., with pointed beard;
behind, long shield with pointed ends;
Rev. Warrior, holding shield and spear,
standing in biga r., driven by naked
charioteer; above, L.HOSTILIVS; below,
SASERN. Æ, 4.12 gm. ↗.
The portrait on the obverse has been identified
as that of the Gallic chieftain, Vercingetorix,
taken prisoner by Caesar at Alesia.
Moneyer: L. Hostilius Saserna.

214 Denarius *c.* 49 BC

Obv. Head of Gallia, with long hair, r.; to l.,
carnyx.
Rev. Diana, standing facing, with r. hand
grasping stag by antlers, and holding
spear in l.; around, L. HOSTILIVS SASERNA.
Æ, 4.15 gm. ↘.
Further reference to Caesar's recent successes in
Gaul.

215 Denarius 49 BC

Obv. Head of Aulus Postumius Albinus r.;
around, A. POSTVMIVS. COS.
Rev. Within wreath of corn-ears, ALBIN
BRVTI.F. Æ, 3.60 gm. ↑.
Decimus Junius Brutus, one of the assassins
of Caesar, had been adopted by Postumius
Albinus, consul in 99 BC. Here, as moneyer, he
uses his adoptive name Postumius Albinus.

216 Denarius *c.* 49 BC

Obv. Head of Pietas with wreath of oak-
    leaves: to l., ⊥II.
Rev. Trophy; at base, captive, with large
    head and hands bound, seated r; l. and r.
    in field CAE SAR. Æ, 3.37 gm. ✓.
It is suggested that ⊥II (52) on the obverse
indicates Caesar's age. The captive on the
reverse may represent the Gallic chief,
Vercingetorix.

217 Denarius *c.* 47 BC

Obv. Head of Medusa, facing; l. and r., a
    coiled snake;
    below, L.PLAVTIVS.
Rev. Aurora, winged, flying r., holding
    palm-branch with wreath, and leading
    the four horses of the sun; below,
    PLANCVS. Æ, 4.13 gm. ↓.
Moneyer: L. Plautius Plancus.

218 Sestertius *c.* 47 BC

Obv. Head of Apollo, laureate, r.; to l.,
    NERVA.
Rev. Victory, advancing r., holding wreath
    and palm-branch; to r., A.LICINI.
    Æ, 0.85 gm. ↑.
A rare late instance of this denomination.
Moneyer: A. Licinius Nerva.

219 Denarius *c.* 47 BC

Obv. Head of Antius Restio, r.; to l., RESTIO.
Rev. Hercules advancing r., raising club in r.
    hand, and holding trophy in l.; over l.
    arm, lion-skin; to r., C. ANTIVS C.F.
    Æ, 3.85 gm. ↓.
A near contemporary portrait of the moneyers'
father, tribune about 74 BC.
Moneyer: C. Antius Restio

220 Quinarius *c.* 47 BC

Obv. Head of Diana, diademed, r.; behind
    shoulder, bow and quiver; to l., C.
    ANTIVS.
Rev. Stag r.; to r., RESTIO. Æ, 2.05 gm. ↖.
An example of the quinarius (half-denarius)
denomination revived in this period.

221 Denarius *c.* 47 BC

Obv. Bust of Venus, diademed, r.; C. CAESAR
    IMP.COS.ITER.
Rev. Trinacrus, standing r., r. foot on prow
    holding triskelis in r. hand; around, A.
    ALLIENVS PRO.COS. Æ, 3.89 gm. ✓.
Allienus, a supporter of Caesar, was governor
of Sicily to which the reverse type makes
allusion.
Moneyer: A. Allienus.

222 Denarius *c.* 47 BC

Obv. Head of Venus, diademed, r.
Rev. Aeneas, advancing l., holding palladium
and carrying his father, Anchises on his
shoulder; to r., CAESAR. Æ, 3.91 gm. ✓.
It is suggested, on grounds of style and fabric,
that this coinage was struck in Greece after
Caesar's defeat of Pompey at Pharsalus. The
types of Venus head and the flight from Troy
allude to the legendary descent of the Julian
family.

223 Denarius *c.* 47 BC

Obv. Head of Jupiter, laureate, r.; around, Q.
METEL PIVS.
Rev. African elephant r.; above, SCIPIO;
below, IMP. Æ, 3.60 gm. ↓.
Coinage struck in Africa where Scipio
commanded the Pompeian troops at Thapsus.

224 Denarius *c.* 47 BC

Obv. Female head, turreted, r., between corn-
ear and caduceus; below, prow to l.,
LEG.PRO.PR; to r., CRASS IVN.
Rev. Trophy between lituus and jug; to l.,
SCIP.IMP; to r., METEL.PIVS.
Æ, 3.89 gm. ↖.

The turreted head probably represents Utica,
the Pompeian base, and possibly mint, in
Africa.
Moneyer: P. Crassus Juniaus.

225 Denarius *c.* 47 BC

Obv. Genius of Africa, lion-headed, standing
front, holding ankh in r. hand; above,
G.T.A.; to l., SCIPIO.IMP; to r., Q.METEL.
PIVS.
Rev. Victory, standing l., holding winged
caduceus and shield; to l., LEG.PRO.PR; to
r., P.CRASSVS.IVN. Æ, 3.91 gm. ↓.
The abbreviation G.T.A. (*Genius tutelaris
Africae*) identifies the obverse type.

226 Denarius *c.* 47 BC

Obv. Head of Africa r., wearing elephant-
skin; to l., SCIPIO IMP; to r., corn-ear and
Q.METELL; below, plough.
Rev. Hercules standing facing, resting l. arm
on club and lion-skin set on rock; to l.,
LEG.F.C.; to r., EPPIVS. Æ, 3.80 gm. ←.
Struck in North Africa by Marcus Eppius,
Pompey's legate in charge of coinage – *legatus
flandum curavit.*

227 Denarius *c.* 47 BC

Obv. Female bust, with slight drapery, r.; to
  l., ROM; below and to r., M.CATO.PRO.PR.
Rev. Victory seated, r., holding patera and
  palm-branch; in ex. VICTRIX.
  Æ, 3.89 gm. ↑.
Cato in North Africa united his forces with
Scipio before the battle of Thapsus. The coin
copies the types of an issue by his namesake in *c.*
90 BC.

228 Denarius *c.* 46 BC

Obv. Bust of Juno Moneta, draped, r.; to l.,
  MONETA.
Rev. Coining instruments – tongs, anvil and
  hammer; above, laureate cap of Vulcan
  and T. CARISIVS; all within a laurel
  wreath. Æ, 3.89 gm. ↑.
The head of Juno Moneta and the illustration of
apparatus of coining are direct allusions to the
office of moneyer.
Moneyer: T. Carisius.

229 Denarius *c.* 46 BC

Obv. Head of the Aphrodisian Sibyl r.
Rev. Sphinx seated r.; to r., T. CARISIVS; in ex.,
  III VIR. Æ, 3.99 gm. →.

The traditional descent of the Julian family
from Venus is alluded to by the type of the
Aphrodisian Sibyl whose oracular quality is
symbolised by the Sphinx.

230 Denarius *c.* 46 BC

Obv. Head of Apollo, laureate, r.; to l.,
  A[pollo].
Rev. Curule chair; above C. CONSIDI; in ex.,
  PAETI. Æ, 4.14 gm. ↘.
The types may refer to a celebration of the *Ludi
Apollinares*.
Moneyer: C. Considius Paetus.

231 Aureus 46 BC

Obv. Head of Pietas, veiled, r.; around, C.
  CAESAR COS.TER.
Rev. Sacrificial implements – lituus, jug, and
  axe; to l. and below, A. HIRTIVS. PR.
  N, 8.07 gm. ←.
A special issue by Hirtius as *praefectus urbi* in
honour of Caesar's quadruple triumph for
victories in Gaul, Egypt, Pontus, and Africa.

232 Denarius *c.* 46 BC

Obv. Bust of Venus, slightly draped, and diademed, l.; to l., small bust of Cupid and lituus; to r., sceptre.

Rev. Trophy of arms; to l., naked captive kneeling; to r., draped female figure seated r.; in ex., CAESAR.
Æ, 3.78 gm. ↗.

Coinage of Caesar for the campaign in Spain.

233 Denarius *c.* 46 BC

Obv. Head of Pompey the Great, bare r.; around, CN.MAGNUS IMP.F.

Rev. Baetica, turreted, standing r. on pile of arms, holding spear and clasping hands with Cnaeus Pompey disembarking from vessel.; on l., PR.Q; in ex., M.MINAT.SABIN. Æ, 3.60 gm. ↙.

This and the following coin, struck by Sabinus, the Pompeian proquaestor in Spain, refer to the successes of Cnaeus Pompey in the Spanish campaign before Caesar's arrival.

234 Denarius *c.* 46 BC

Obv. Head of Pompey the Great, bare, r.; around, CN. MAGNS IMP.

Rev. Baetica, turreted, standing r,; Cnaeus Pompey standing r., receiving shield from Tarraco, kneeling l.; in ex., M. MINAT. SABI. Æ, 3.74 gm. ↘.

235 Denarius *c.* 45 BC

Obv. Head of Triumphus, laureate, r.; behind, trophy; below, TRIVMPVS.

Rev. She-wolf r., placing brand on brazier; to r., eagle standing l.; above, CELSVS III VIR; in ex., L. PAPIVS. Æ, 4.14 gm. ↓.

The obverse continues the celebration of Caesar's triumph; the reverse illustrates a legend connected with the foundation by Aeneas of Lanuvium with which the moneyer's family was connected.

Moneyer: L. Papius Celsus.

236 Denarius *c.* 45 BC

Obv. Head of Libertas, diademed, r.; to l., LIBERTAS.

Rev. Rostra surmounted by sella; above, PALIKANVS. Æ, 4.06 gm. ↙.

The types may refer to the successful efforts of the tribune M. Lollius Palikanus to secure the restoration of the tribunes' privileges amoved by Sulla.

237 Denarius *c.* 45 BC

Obv. Head of Apollo Soranus, diademed, r.;
    above, star; to l.; double-headed adze
    and ACISCVLVS.
Rev. Owl with helmeted human head, and
    carrying two spears and shield, r.; in ex.,
    L. VALERIVS; all in laurel-wreath.
    Æ, 3.67 gm. ↗.
The types allude to the legendary early history
of the moneyer's family in Falerii in Etruria.
Moneyer: L. Valerius Acisculus.

238 Denarius *c.* 45 BC

Obv. Head of Jupiter, laureate, r.; to l.,
    double-headed adze and ACISCVLVS; all
    within laurel-wreath.
Rev. Anguipedic giant facing, holding
    thunderbolt in r. hand; in ex.,
    L.VALERIVS. Æ, 4.17 gm. ↙.
The types, particularly the anguipedic giant,
symbolic of sedition, could refer to Caesar's
triumph over his opponents.

239 Gold quinarius *c.* 45 BC

Obv. Bust of Victory, winged, r.; around, C.
    CAES. DIC. TER.
Rev. Jug with handle; to l. and r.; L. PLANC
    PRAEF.VRB. A͞V, 4.08 gm. ↖.

A special issue by Plancus as *praefectus urbi*. A
rare instance of this denomination.

240 As *c.* 45 BC

Obv. Bust of Victory, winged, draped, r.; to
    l., CAESAR. DIC. TER.
Rev. Minerva, helmeted, draped, r., carrying
    trophy over shoulder in r. hand, and
    spears and Gorgon shield in l.; at foot,
    serpent; around, C. CLOVI. PRAEF.
    Æ, 15.29 gm. ↑.
Another part of the special issue of the year by
Clovius as *praefectus uvbi*.

241 Denarius *c.* 45 BC

Obv. Head of Pompey the Great, bare, l.;
    around, SEX MAGNUS SA͡L IMP.
Rev. Pietas standing front, head l., holding
    branch and sceptre; to r., PIETAS.
    Æ, 3.30 gm. ↓.
Coinage struck by Sextus Pompey in Spain
after his proclamation as imperator (*imperator
salutatus*).

242   As *c.* 45 BC

Obv. Janiform head of Pompey laureate;
   above MAGNVS.
Rev. Prow r.; above, PIUS; below, IMP.
   Æ, 15.94 gm. ↗.
The traditional types of the *as* revived for this
issue, but with the obverse transformed into a
portrait.

243   Denarius January, 44 BC

Obv. Head of Venus, diademed, r.; to l., L.
   BVCA.
Rev. Sulla's dream; Sulla reclining r.; to r.,
   Selene veiled, with crescent on head,
   and holding torch; behind, Victory
   standing facing, holding palm-branch.
   Æ, 3.71 gm.↓.
Plutarch relates that Sulla, marching on Rome
in 82 BC, saw in a dream a vision of Selene who
placed in his hands thunder to destroy his
enemies.
Moneyer: L. Aemilius Buca.

244   Denarius January, 44 BC

Obv. Head of Caesar, laureate, r.; behind,
   lituus; around, CAESAR. DICT QVART.
Rev. Juno Sospita, wearing goat-skin head-
   dress and holding spear, in biga r.; in ex.,
   M. METTIVS. Æ, 3.92 gm. ↓.
With the possible exception of the gold stater
of Flamininus (No. 76 above) this is the earliest
instance of a coin portrait of a living Roman.
Moneyer: M. Mettius.

245   Denarius February, 44 BC

Obv. Head of Caesar, laureate, r.; around,
   CAESAR. DICT PERPETVO.
Rev. Winged caduceus and fasces in saltire; in
   angles, globe, clasped hands, axe, and L.
   BUCA. Æ, 3.90 gm. ←.
By the Lupercalia on 15 February Caesar's title
in use was *Dictator Perpetuus*.
Moneyer: L. Aemilius Buca.

246   Denarius February–March, 44 BC

Obv. Head of Caesar, laureate, veiled, r.;
   around, CAESAR DICT. PERPETVO.
Rev. Venus standing l., holding. in r. hand,
   Victory, and in l., sceptre resting on
   shield; around, P. SEPVLLIVS MACER.
   Æ, 3.85 gm. ↓.
The veiled portrait is that of Caesar as Pontifex
Maximus.
Moneyer: P. Sepullius Macer.

247 Denarius March, 44 BC

Obv. Head of Caesar, laureate, veiled, r.;
between lituus and apex; around,
CAESAR PARENS PATRIAE.
Rev. Inscription C. COSSVTIVS MARIDIANVS
arranged in form of cross; in angles A A
A F F . ᴭ, 7.61 gm. →.

The final version of Caesar's titulature before
the assassination on the Ides of March. The
exceptional weight and large flan suggest that
this may be in the nature of a trial-piece.
Moneyer: C. Cossutius Maridianus.

248 Denarius 44 BC

Obv. Head of Caesar, laureate, r.; to l., bowl
and lituus; to r. CAESAR.IMP.
Rev. Venus standing r., holding Victory on r.
hand, and sceptre in l.; l. elbow rests on
shield; to l., H; to r., M.METTIVS.
ᴭ, 4.06 gm. ↗.

Part of a special military issue for Caesar as
imperator.
Moneyer: M. Mettius.

249 Denarius After 15 March, 44 BC

Obv. Head of Mark Antony, bearded, veiled,
r.; to l., jug; to r., lituus.
Rev. Two horses galloping r., on nearer,
mounted horseman holding whip; to r.,
wreath and palm-branch; above,
P.SEPVLLIVS; in ex., MACER.
ᴭ, 4.27 gm. ↖.

The reverse used by Macer with Caesar's final
titulature, *parens patriae*, was further employed
with the portrait of Antony as an augur. The
beard indicates mourning for Caesar's death.
Moneyer: P. Sepullius Macer.

250 Denarius After 15 March 44 BC

Obv. Tetrastyle temple with closed doors; in
tympanum, a globe; around CLEMENTIAE
CAESARIS.
Rev. As No. 249. ᴭ, 3.86 gm. →.

Another combination using Macer's *desultor*
reverse forms part of Caesar's posthumous
coinage.

6 The Triumvirate: Antony and Octavian 43–31 BC

The struggle for power which lasted from the death of Caesar until the emergence of Octavian as the sole ruler of the Roman world after the defeat of Antony and Cleopatra at Actium in 31 BC is well reflected in the coinage. The still extensive series of silver denarii were supplemented by more frequent and abundant coinage of gold aurei, and, towards the end of the period, bronze coinage began to form a more significant part of the coinage pattern.

Italy, and the mint of Rome, in effect never passed out of Octavian's control and struck for him and for the other members of the triumvirate as long as good relations were maintained. Imperatorial coinage, produced at centres other than Rome, which had been a feature of the successive power struggles from the time of Sulla, now played an even larger role. Such issues were produced either by or for the members of the triumvirate from mints in the provinces over which they, at various times, exercised control. Other imperatorial coinage was struck by the continuing opposition of the Pompeians, by or for Brutus and Cassius in Greece and Asia, and by Sextus Pompey in Sicily.

In this period the long tradition that coin types were confined to allusions to and illustration of events and personalities in the history of the moneyer's family practically came to an end. More and more obverse tended to show the portrait and title of the person – triumvir or imperator – by whose authority the coin was struck, setting a fashion which was to be developed and perpetuated in the coinage of the empire.

251 Denarius 43 BC

Obv. Head of Caesar, laureate, r.
Rev. Pax standing l., holding caduceus in r. hand and sceptre in l., around, L. FLAMINIVS III·VIR. Æ, 3.58 gm. ↑.
Moneyer: L. Flaminius Chilo.

252 Denarius 43 BC

Obv. Bust of Acca Larentia, draped, head bound with fillet, r.; around, P·ACCOLEIVS LARISCOLVS.
Rev. Three caryatid statues of the *nymphae querquetulanae* supporting a beam from which issue five trees. Æ, 3.99 gm. ↓.
The obverse bust has been identified as that of Acca Larentia, said to be the wife of the shepherd Faustulus, and the nurse of Romulus and Remus.
Moneyer: P. Accoleius Lariscolus.

253   Denarius 43 BC

Obv. Eagle with spread wings, standing r. on thunderbolt; above PETILLIVS; below, CAPITOLINVS.

Rev. Hexastyle temple; each side of pediment is decorated with horse's head and standing figure, and with half-figure of horseman at apex; in tympanum, seated figure of Jupiter; l. and r. in field, S F (*sacris faciundis*). Æ, 3.84 gm. ↗.

A representation of the Capitoline temple of Jupiter.

Moneyer: Petillius Capitolinus.

254   Aureus *c.* 43 BC

Obv. Bust of Africa, draped, and wearing elephant's scalp head-dress, r.

Rev. Crested helmet on curule chair with legs decorated with winged figures; on r., PR (*praefecti*); on l., SC (*senatus consulto*); above, L. CESTIVS; in ex., C. NORBA. Æ, 8.03 gm. ↖.

Moneyers: L. Cestius and C. Norbanus.

255   Aureus *c.* 43 BC

Obv. Bust of Sibyl, draped, head bound with fillet, r.; to r., PR; above, C. NORBANVS; below, L. CESTIVS.

Rev. Cybele, turreted, holding patera in r. hand, and resting l. elbow on tympanum, seated r. in car drawn by two lions; to l., SC. Æ, 8.10 gm. ↖.

256   Denarius 43 BC

Obv. Male bust r. (Genius of Macedonia), wearing chlamys and cap; around, C. ANTONIVS·M·F· PRO·COS.

Rev. Two simpula and an axe; below, PONTIFEX. Æ, 3.96 gm. ↑.

Issued by Caius Antonius, brother of Marcus, elected pontif in 44 BC and allotted the province of Macedonia where he was captured and put to death by Brutus.

257   Aureus *c.* 43 BC

Obv. Head of Octavian r.; around, C· CAESAR.COS·PONT·AVG·

Rev. Head of Caesar, laureate, r.; around, C· CAESAR · DICT · PERP · PON · MAX. Æ, 8.00 gm. ↗.

Issued by Octavian after his election as consul in August 43 BC and before the formation of the triumvirate.

258 Denarius *c.* 43 BC

Obv. Lituus, jug, and raven; below, M.
ANTON.IMP.

Rev. Apex, axe, aspergillum and simpulum;
to l.; and above, M· LEPID · IMP.
Æ, 3.54 gm. ↙.

An imperatorial coinage by Antony in Gaul
before the institution of the triumvirate.

259 Denarius *c.* 43 BC

Obv. Head of Antony, r.; to l., lituus; to r.,
M. ANTON · IMP.

Rev. Head of Caesar, laureate, r.; to l., jug;
to r., CAESAR D[IC]. Æ, 3.67 gm. ↙.

The presence of RPC (*reipublicae conistituendae*),
part of the formula associated with the coinage
of the triumvirate, on some coins of this
imperatorial coinage by Antony in Gaul,
suggests that the issue was in progress when the
triumvirate was formed in November 43 BC.

260 Aureus 42 BC

Obv. Head of Antony bare, r.; around, M·
ANTONIVS · III·VIR · R.P.C. (*triumvir
reipublicae constituendae*).

Rev. Anteon, seated l. on rocks with shield at
side, and holding spear in r. hand and
parazonium in l.; around, L · REGVLVS·
IIII · VIR · A · P · F (*quatuorvir auro publico
feriundo*). ℵ, 7.98 gm. ↗.

The moneyer Livineius Regulus struck a
coinage with portraits of each of the
triumvirate instituted in November 43 BC,
with reverses relating to the origin of their
families. On this coin, the origin of the
Antonian family is traced from Anteon, a son
of Hercules.

261 Aureus 42 BC

Obv. Head of Lepidus, bare, r.; around M·
LEPIDVS· III· VIR· R·P·C;

Rev. The Vestal virgin, Aemilia, standing l.,
holding simpulum in r. hand and
transverse sceptre in l.; around,
L·REGVLVS · IIII·VIR · A·P·F.
ℵ, 7.98 gm. ↓.

A component of the issue described under No.
260. The reverse here refers to the origin of the
Aemilian family.

262   Aureus 42 BC

Obv. Head of Octavian, bare, r.; around, C.
CAESAR. III · VIR· R·P·C·
Rev. Aeneas advancing r., carrying on his
shoulder, his father, Anchises; around, L
REGVLVS·IIII·VÍR·A·P·F. ℕ, 8.30 gm. ↑.
A further part of the triumvival issue together
with Nos. 260–1. The reverse, showing the
flight from Troy, refers to the descent of the
Julian family from Venus through Aeneas.

263   Denarius 42 BC

Obv. Head of Lucius Regulus, the praetor,
bare, r.
Rev. Combat with wild beasts; in ex., L·
REGVLVS. ℛ, 4.30 gm. ↑.
Another obverse in the series with the same
type, the head of Lucius Regulus, the
moneyer's father, but inscribed REGVLVS PR.
shows that the series was issued by Livineius
Regulus in his capacity of *praefectus urbi*.

264   Aureus 42 BC

Obv. Head of Antony, bare, r.; around
M·ANTONIVS. III·VIR· R·P·C.

Rev. Genius, winged, radiate standing l., foot
on globe; holding caduceus and cornucopiae; on shoulder, bow and quiver;
to l., eagle on cippus; to r., shield;
around, P·CLODIVS M·F·IIII·VIR·A·P·F.
ℕ, 8.02 gm. ↖.
A pantheistic reverse type combining the
attributes of Sol, Mercury, Mars, Victory,
Fortuna and Jupiter.
Moneyer: P. Clodius.

265   Denarius 42 BC

Obv. Bust of Sol, radiate, draped facing l.
Rev. Platform with balustrade inscribed
CLOACIN; on it, two statues of Venus
Cloacina; to l., a flight of steps; above,
L·MUSSIDIVS·LONGVS. ℛ, 3.73 gm. ↖.
A representation of the shrine of Venus
Cloacina in front of the Basilica Aemilia in the
Forum.
Moneyer: L. Mussidius Longus.

266   Aureus 42 BC

Obv. Bust of Roma in winged and crested
helmet, l., and holding spear and shield.
Rev. Winged Nemesis standing l., pulling
forward fold of robe from breast; to r.,
C·VIBIVS; to l.; VARVS. ℕ, 8.01 gm. ↙.
Moneyer: C. Vibius Varus.

267 Aureus 42 BC

Obv. Head of Antony, bare, r.; to l., lituus;
  around M·ANTONIVS·III·VIR·R·P·C.
Rev. Head of Lepidus, bare, r.; behind,
  simpulum and aspergillum; around,
  M·LEPIDVS·III·VIR·R·P·C. N, 8.13 gm. ↗.
As this and the following coin both have the
portrait of Antony they form part of an
imperatorial coinage struck by Antony in Gaul
after the formation of the triumvirate.

268 Aureus 42 BC

Obv. As No. 267.
Rev. Head of Octavian, head bare, r.;
  around, C·CAESAR·III·VIR·R·P·C.
  N, 7.94 gm. ↗.
A companion piece to No. 267.

269 Aureus 42 BC

Obv. Head of Lucius Junius Brutus, bare, r.;
  around, L·BRVTVS·PRIM·COS (*Primus
  consul*); all within oak-wreath.
Rev. Head of Marcus Junius Brutus, bare, r.;
  above, M·BRVTVS IMP; below, COSTA LEG;
  all within oak-wreath. N, 8.15 gm. ↑.

Imperatorial coinage probably struck in Greece
for Brutus by his legate, Costa. The obverse
portrait is that of Brutus's ancestor, the first
consul elected after the expulsion of the kings
in 509 BC.

270 Denarius 42 BC

Obv. Head of Apollo, laureate, r.
Rev. Trophy; at foot, seated l. and r. a female
  and a male captive; at sides and below,
  Q·CAEPIO BRVTVS IMP. AR, 3.95 gm. ↑.
Imperatorial coinage of Brutus in Greece.

271 Denarius 42 BC

Obv. Head of Apollo, laureate, r.; around,
  COSTA LEG.
Rev. Trophy; around, BRVTVS IMP.
  AR, 3.86 gm. ↑.
Another issue by Brutus's legate, Costa.

272 Aureus 42 BC

Obv. Head of Brutus, bare, r.; to l., BRVTVS;
to r., IMP.

Rev. Combined military and naval trophy; in
field l., L (*libertas*); to l., CASCA; to r.,
LONGVS. *N*, 7.99 gm. ↗.

Eastern imperatorial coinage for Brutus by
Casca who may have been his fleet commander.

273 Denarius 42 BC

Obv. Head of Neptune, laureate, r.; below,
trident; to l., CASCA; LONGVS.

Rev. Victory advancing r., holding palm-
branch and broken diadem; below,
broken sceptre; to l., BRVTVS; to r., IMP.
R, 4.05 gm. ↑.

A further part of the imperatorial coinage
issued by Casca. The broken diadem and fillet
symbolise the anti-tyrannical motivation of
Brutus, as does the initial L for *libertas* on the
aureus, No. 274.

274 Denarius 42 BC

Obv. Head of Brutus, bare, r.; to l.,
L·PLAET·CEST; above, BRVT; to r., IMP.

Rev. Cap of liberty between two daggers;
below, EID·MAR (*Eidibus martiis*).
R, 3.80 gm. ↑.

Another issue in Greece by one of Brutus's
officers, Plaetorius Cestianus. The reverse
declares the object of the conspiracy against
Caesar, the assertion of liberty, the means of the
assassination, and its date, the Ides of March.

275 Aureus 42 BC

Obv. Head of Libertas, laureate, r.; to l.,
C·CASSI·IMP.

Rev. Aplustre with branches ending in roses;
to l., M· SERVILIVS; to r. LEG.
N, 8.08 gm. ↙.

Coinage for Cassius by Servilius, one of his
fleet commanders. The reverse, and specifically
the roses, alludes to the defeat of the Rhodian
fleet.

276 Denarius 42 BC

Obv. Head of Libertas, laureate, r.; to l.,
M·SERVILIVS; to r., LEG.

Rev. Trophy; to l., Q·CAEPIO; to r., BRVTVS
IMP. *R*, 3.92 gm. ↓.

Struck in the East by Servilius as a legate of
Brutus as part of the imperatorial coinage in the
period before Philippi.

277 **Denarius** 42 BC

Obv. As No. 275, but C·CASSEI·IMP.
Rev. Crab holding an aplustre in its claws;
below, a loosened diadem and a rose; to
l., M·SERVILIVS; to r., LEG.
Ⱥ, 3.84 gm. ↓.

The rose refers to Rhodes whose fleet was
defeated off Cos symbolised by the crab.

278 **Denarius** 42 BC

Obv. Head of Neptune, r.; to l., trident.
Rev. Trophy before which male figure,
standing r., holding sword raises kneeling female figure; in ex., MVRCVS IMP.
Ⱥ, 3.40 gm. ↑.

Imperatorial coinage in the East. The reverse
may refer to Murcus's successful capture of
Apamaea from Caecilius Bassus and the
obverse to his success against Dolabella as
praefectus classis of Cassius.

279 **Denarius** 42 BC

Obv. Head of Jupiter Ammon l.

Rev. Cornuficius in augur's dress and holding
lituus, standing l., crowned by Juno
Sospita, in goat-skin head-dress, standing l., and holding spear and shield
surmounted by a raven; around and in
ex., Q·CORNVFICI AVGVR·IMP.
Ⱥ, 3.50 gm. ↙.

Coinage issued by Cornuficius in Africa
where, having sided with Sextus Pompey, he
was eventually defeated by the triumviral
governor, T. Sextius, near Utica.

280 **Denarius** 42 BC

Obv. Head of Pompey the Great, bare, r.; to
l., jug; to r., lituus; around
MAG·PIVS·IMP·ITER.
Rev. Neptune standing l., foot on prow, and
holding aplustre, between the Catanian
brothers Anapias and Amphinomus,
carrying their parents on their shoul-
ders; above and in ex.,
PRAEF·ORAE·MARIT· ET·CLAS·EX·S·C.
(*praefectus orae maritimae et classis ex
senatus consulto*). Ⱥ, 3.69 gm. →.

Sextus Pompey, appointed *praefectus* after his
reconciliation with the triumvirs, seized Sicily
after relations were ruptured. The occasion of
this coinage was his defeat of Salvidienus sent
to dislodge him in 42 BC.

281   Aureus 42 BC

Obv. Head of Sextus Pompey, bare, r.;
around, MAG·PIVS·IMP·ITER; all within
oak-wreath.

Rev. Heads of Pompey the Great and Cnaeus
Pompey, both bare, facing one another;
to l., lituus; to r., tripod; above and
below, PRAEF·CLAS·ET·ORAE·MARI
T·EX·S·C· Ν, 8.09 gm. ↙.

Another part of the coinage issued by Sextus
Pompey in the same circumstances as No. 281.

282   Aureus 41 BC

Obv. Bust of Flora with wreath of leaves and
flowers, draped, r.; to l., lily; to r.,
C·CLODIVS C·F·

Rev. Vestal virgin, Claudia Quinta, veiled,
seated l., holding bowl; to r., VESTALIS.
Ν, 8.08 gm. ↙.

Moneyer: C. Clodius.

283   Denarius 41 BC

Obv. Head of Numonius Vaala, bare, r.;
around C·NVMONIVS VAALA.

Rev. Warrior armed with shield and sword
attacking a *vallum*, defended by two
soldiers; in ex., VAALA. Ҋ, 4.05 gm. ↗.

The types presumably portray an ancestor of
the moneyer, C. Numonius Vaala, and the
action which earned him his cognomen.

284   Denarius 41 BC

Obv. Head of Quintus Arrius, bare, r.;
around, M·ARRIVS·SECVNDVS.

Rev. Spear between wreath and phalerae.
Ҋ, 3.81 gm. ↖.

The portrait has been identified as that of
Quintus Arrius, possibly the moneyer's father,
who as praetor in Sicily in 72 BC, was
concerned with the suppression of the revolt of
Spartacus.

285   Denarius 41 BC

Obv. Head of Servius Sulpicius Rufus, bare,
r.; around, L·SERVIVS RVFVS·

Rev. The Dioscuri, armed with spear and
parazonium, standing facing.
Ҋ, 4.10 gm. ↘.

The types are associated with the incident
described under No. 286.

286   Aureus 41 BC

Obv. Conjoined heads of the Dioscuri, laureate, r.; around, L·SERVIVS RVFVS.
Rev. View of Tusculum, with gateway inscribed TVSCVL. *N*, 8.11 gm. ←.
The types refer to the relief in 374 BC by Servius Sulpicius Rufus of Tusculum where the citizens had sought refuge in the temple of the Dioscuri in the citadel.

287 Aureus 41 BC

Obv. Head of Antony, bare, r.; around ANT·AVG· IMP III·V·R·P·C.
Rev. Pietas standing l., holding rudder and cornucopiae; at foot, l., a stork; below, PIETAS COS. *N*, 8.05 gm. ↑.
Coinage for the Antonian party in Cisalpine Gaul supporting Lucius Antonius who, having taken up the cause of those dispossessed by Octavian's settlement of his veterans, was besieged in Perugia. Lucius Antonius, consul in 41 BC, adopted the cognomen Pietas to mark his support for his brother, Mark Antony.

288 Denarius 42 BC

Obv. Head of Antony, bare, r.; around, M·ANTONI IMP.
Rev. Distyle temple enclosing medallion bearing bust of Sol, radiate and draped; at sides and below, III VIR R·P·C· *R*, 4.06 gm. ←.
Imperatorial coinage of Antony in Gaul.

289 Denarius 41 BC

Obv. Head of Octavian, bare, r., around, C·CAESAR·III·VIR·R·P·C.
Rev. Equestrian statue of Octavian r.; in ex., S.C. *R*, 3.53 gm. ←.
Coinage of the Octavian party in Cisalpine Gaul in the Perusine incident (No. 287). Equestrian statues of Octavian were set up in Rome by senatorial decree in 43 BC.

290 Denarius 41 BC

Obv. As No. 289.
Rev. Equestrian statue of Octavian galloping l.; in ex., POPVL IVSSV. *R*, 3.95 gm. ↘.
Part of the issue described under No. 289.

291 Aureus 41 BC

Obv. Head of Domitius Ahenobarbus, bare, r.; to r., AHENOBAR.
Rev. Perspective view of tetrastyle temple; to l. and r., above, NE PT; at sides and below, CN·DOMITIVS·L·F·IMP. *N*, 8.16 gm. ←.
Ahenobarbus, a naval commander of Brutus, was saluted imperator after his success in the battle of Brundisium in 42 BC. This coinage was issued when, after Philippi, he operated independently in the Ionian sea for some time.

292 Denarius 4I BC

Obv. Head of Lucius Domitius Ahenobarbus, bare, r., to r., AHENOBAR.

Rev. Prow r., surmounted by military trophy; at sides and below, CN·DOMITIVS·IMP. Æ, 3.92 gm. ↙.

Part of the issue described under No. 291. The portrait on the obverse is of Lucius Domitius to whom the Dioscuri announced the Roman success at Lake Regillus in 496 BC. They confirmed their report by stroking his hair and beard which changed to a brassy colour, the incident which attached the cognomen Ahenobarbus to the Domitian family.

293 Denarius 4I BC

Obv. Head of Antony, bare, r.; around M·ANT·IMP·AVG·III·VIR·R·P·C M·NERVA·PROQ·P.

Rev. Head of Lucius Antonius, bare, r.; around, L.ANTONIVS COS. Æ, 4.07 gm. ↑.

Struck by Nerva as *proquaestor propraetore* of Antony, possibly when Antony was in Asia after Philippi in 4I BC when Lucius was consul.

294 Denarius 4I BC

Obv. Head of Labienus, bare, r.; around Q·LABIENVS·PARTHICVS·IMP.

Rev. Horse, bridled and saddled, r.; bowcase attached to saddle. Æ, 3.78 gm. ↘.

Labienus, sent by Brutus and Cassius to seek aid from Orodes of Parthia, after Philippi joined with the Parthians in attacking the Roman provinces in Asia.

295 Denarius 40 BC

Obv. Head of Caesar, laureate, r.

Rev. Calf walking l.; l. and r., S.C; above, Q.VOCONIVS; below, VITVLVS·Q·DESIGN. Æ, 3.54 gm. ↘.

The reverse type of a calf, as well as being a pun on the moneyer's name, may also contain an allusion to Octavian's settlement of his veterans on the land.

Moneyer: Q. Voconius Vitulus.

296 Denarius 40 BC

Obv. Head of Caesar, laureate, r.

Rev. Two standards, a plough, and a sceptre; above, TI·SEMPRON; below, GRACCVS; to r., III VIR.; to l., Q·DESIG. Æ, 3.83 gm. ↘.

The reverse type makes a more explicit allusion to veteran land settlement (*cf.* No. 295).

Moneyer: Ti. Sempronius Graccus.

297 Aureus 40 BC

Obv. Head of Octavian, bare, r., around,
CAESAR IMP.
Rev. Head of Antony, bare, r.; around,
ANTONIVS IMP. A⁄, 8.31 gm. ↘.
The occasion of this coinage was the renewal of
friendly relations between Octavian and
Antony, marked by Antony's marriage to
Octavia (*cf.* Nos 301–3).

298 Denarius 40 BC

Obv. Head of Lepidus, bare, r.; around,
LEPIDVS·PON·MAX·III·VͶR·R·P·C.
Rev. Head of Octavian, bare, r.; around,
CAESAR·IMP·III·VIR·R·P·C.
Æ, 3.74 gm. ↘.
Lepidus, virtually excluded by the other
triumvirs after Philippi, was allowed by
Octavian to take possession of Africa after the
Perusine war in 40 BC.

299 Denarius 39 BC

Obv. Head of Antony, bare, r.; to l., lituus;
around, M·ANͶT·III·V·R·P·C.
Rev. Jupiter, standing front, head r., holding
sceptre and olive-branch; around,
P·VENͶTIDI·PONͶT·IMP. Æ, 3.67 gm. ↗.

Struck by Ventidius probably in the East when,
under Antony's command, he opposed the
attacks of Labienus (*cf.* No. 294).

300 Denarius 39 BC

Obv. Head of Hercules, r.; to l., OSCA.
Rev. Priestly emblems – apex, securis,
aspergillum and simpulum; below and
to r., DOM·COS·ITER·IMP.
Æ, 3.91 gm. ↙.
Struck in Spain by Domitius Calvinus for his
campaign against the Cerretani.

301 Cistophoric tetradrachm 39 BC

Obv. Head of Antony, with ivy wreath, r.;
below lituus; around
M·ANTONIVS·IMP·COS·DESIG·ITER ET TERT,
all in wreath of ivy and berries.
Rev. Cista mystica surmounted by bust of
Octavia r.; all between two snakes; to l.,
III·VIR·; to r., R·P·C· Æ, 12.24 gm. ↑.
Struck at Ephesus to commemorate the
marriage of Antony and Octavia following the
renewal of friendly relations between Octavian
and Antony at Brundisium in 40 BC (*cf.* No.
297).

302   Aureus 38 BC

Obv. Head of Antony, bare, r.; around,
M·ANTONIVS·M·F·M·N·AVGVR·IMP·TER.
Rev. Head of Octavia, r.; around,
COS·DESIGN·ITER·ET·TER·III·VIR·R·P·C.
N, 8.06 gm. ↗.
Another coinage, possibly struck at Athens,
celebrating the marriage of Antony and
Octavia.

303   Dupondius 38 BC

Obv. Heads of Antony on l. and Octavia on
r., facing one another. [M·ANT̂·IMP·TER]
COS·DESIG·ITER [ET·TER·III·VIR·R·P·C·].
Rev. Two galleys sailing r.; to l. and r., cap of
the Dioscuri; below, [B]; around, [M·OP]
PIVS·CAPITO·PRO·P [R·PRAEF·CLASS·F·C].
Æ, 17.36 gm. ↙.
A bronze coinage on the same occasion as No.
302 with naval types was struck (F.C. = *flandum
curavit*) by Oppius Capito, Antony's pro-
praetor and prefect of his fleet.

304   Denarius 38 BC

Obv. Heads of Caesar, laureate, and Octavian,
bare, facing one another; to l.,
DIVOS·IVLIVS; to r., DIVI·F.
Rev. In two lines across field, M·AGRIPPA·CO
[S] / DESIG· Æ, 3.99 gm. →.
Issued by Agrippa in Gaul in this year.

305   Sestertius(?) 38 BC

Obv. Head of Octavian, bare, r.; to r.,
CAESAR; to l., DIVI·F
Rev. Head of Caesar, laureate, r.; to r.,
DIVOS; to l., IVLIVS. Æ, 23.34 gm. ↖.
Another part of Agrippa's issues in Gaul. The
earliest appearance of the sestertius which was
to become a regular part of Augustus's imperial
coinage.

306   Denarius 38 BC

Obv. Head of Neptune, diademed, r.; to l.,
trident; around, MAG·PIVS·IMP·ITER.
Rev. Naval trophy set on anchor; in place
of the arms, prow and aplustre; at
bottom of trophy, heads of Scylla and
Charybdis; above, trident; around,
PRAEF·CLAS·ET·ORAE·MARIT·EX·S·C·
Æ, 4.04 gm. ↖.
The reverse type refers to Sextus Pompey's
initial naval successes off Cumae in 38 BC.

307 **Denarius** 38 BC

Obv. Pharos of Messana surmounted by
helmeted Neptune holding trident and
rudder and placing foot on prow; in
front, galley l., with legionary eagle at
stern and, at stem, grappling iron,
aplustre, flag-staff, and trident; around,
MAG·PIVS·IMP·ITER.

Rev. Scylla wielding rudder; around
PRAEF·CLAS·ET·ORAE·MARIT·EX·S·C·
Æ, 3.87, gm. ↘.

A further allusion to Sextus Pompey's
successes.

308 **Denarius** 38 BC

Obv. Head of Pompey the Great, bare, r.;
below, dolphin; to r., trident; to l.,
NEPTVNI.

Rev. Galley r., above to l., star; below,
Q·NASSIDIVS. Æ, 3.99 gm. ↘.

Nassidius, earlier recorded as a Pompeian
supporter, may, his types suggest, have
participated in the naval battles of 38 BC.

309 **Sestertius (?)** 37 BC

Obv. Head of Agrippa, bare, l.; around,
M·AGRIPPA PRAE [MAR ET] CLAS·PRAEF.

Rev. Triskelis with winged Medusa head at
centre; around CAESAR III·VIR·R·P·C.
Æ, 27.5 gm. ↗.

In 37 BC Agrippa succeeded to the office of high
admiral. The coin has been attributed to his
naval headquarters at Puteoli.

310 **Denarius** 36 BC

Obv. Head of Antony bare, r.; around,
ANTONIVS·AVGVR·COS·DES·ITER·ET·TERT.

Rev. Armenian tiara; behind, in saltire, bow
and arrow; around, IMP·TERTIO·III·
VIR·R·P·C. Æ, 3.89 gm. ↘.

The reverse refers to Artavasdes, king of
Armenia, in alliance with whom Antony in
this year embarked on his attempted invasion
of Parthia.

311 **Aureus** 36 BC

Obv. Head of Octavian, bare, r.; around,
IMP·CAESAR·DIVI·F·III·VIR·R·P·C.

Rev. Tetrastyle temple enclosing statue of
Caesar; in pediment, star; on architrave,
DIVO IVL; to l., lighted altar; around,
COS·ITER·ET·TER·DESIG. N, 8.06 gm. ↘.

The issue of this coinage has been attributed to
Statilius Taurus, Octavian's legate in Africa
after Naulochus. The temple on the reverse is
possibly that of Divus Julius being constructed
in the Forum.

312 Aureus 36 BC

Obv. Head of Octavian, bare, l.
Rev. Decorated triumphal quadriga l.,
    surmounted by small quadriga with
    horses galloping; in ex., CAESAR DIVI·F.
    Ȧ, 7.72 gm. ↓.
Coinage of Octavian in Rome to celebrate his
ovation after the defeat of Sextus Pompey at
Naulochus.

313 Denarius 36 BC

Obv. Head of Octavian, bare, r.
Rev. Venus Victrix standing l., resting l. arm
    on column, and holding sceptre and
    helmet; to l., shield; across field, CAESAR
    DIVI·F. Ȧ, 3.55 gm. ↗.
Another part of Octavian's coinage at Rome
after Naulochus. Venus on the reverse, as well
as alluding to the origin of the Julian family, is
appropriately represented in this coinage as
Venus Victrix.

314 Aureus 34 BC

Obv. Head of Antony, bare, r.; around,
    ANTON·AVG·IMP·III·COS·DES·III·III·V·R·P·C.

Rev. Head of Mark Antony the younger,
    bare, r.; around, M·ANTONIVS·M·F·F.
    Ȧ, 7.97 gm. ↙.
At the date suggested by the titulature Antony
in the East was engaged in his Armenian
campaign.

315 Denarius 32 BC.

Obv. Head of Antony, bare, r.; to l., an
    Armenian tiara; around,
    ANTONI·ARMEN[IA] DEVICTA.
Rev. Bust of Cleopatra, diademed, draped, r.,
    to l., stem of prow; around,
    CLEOPATRAE·REGINAE·REGVM·FILIORVM·
    REGVM. Ȧ, 3.90 gm. ↑.
The obverse inscription and the tiara refer to
Antony's recent conquest of Armenia, and the
reverse legend to the honours decreed by
Antony to Cleopatra's sons, the 'Donations of
Alexandria'.

316 Aureus 31 BC

Obv. Galley r., with standard at prow; above
    ANT AVG; below, III VIR R·P·C.
Rev. Legionary eagle between two stan-
    dards.; around COHRTIVM PRAETORIARVM.
    Ȧ, 8.06 gm. ↓.
In the period before the battle of Actium
Antony produced a coinage in gold and silver
with types honouring both his naval and
military forces. The unit referred to here, the
cohortes praetoriae, was the commander's
bodyguard.

317 Denarius 31 BC

Obv. As No. 316.
Rev. As No. 316, but below in field LEG PRI.
ℛ, 3.78 gm. ↓
The legion honoured is usually indicated by a numeral after the word LEG, e.g. LEG II but in the case of the First Legion here the ordinal is used.

318 Denarius 31 BC

Obv. As No. 316.
Rev. As No. 316, but above, LEG·XII. ANTIQVAE. ℛ, 3.55 gm. ↓.
For a few legions some reverses record additionally the legionary cognomen.

319 Denarius 31 BC

Obv. Head of Jupiter Ammon r., around, M·ANTO COS III IMP IIII.
Rev. Legionary eagle between two standards; in field, LEG VIII; above SCARPVS; to l., IMP. ℛ, 3.11 gm. ↖.
Coinage in Cyrene of Scarpus in command of four legions and a supporter of Antony, the reverse type of whose legionary coinage is copied here.

Concordance

Almost all the references are to catalogue numbers in the several sections of the *British Museum Catalogue of Coins of the Roman Republic*. The letters preceding the catalogue numbers indicate the following sections: *Af* – Africa; *AG* – *aes grave*; *AS* – aes signatum; *Cyr* – Cyrenaica; *E* – East; *G* – Gaul; *It* – Italy; *R* – Rome; *RG* – Romano-Campanian; *Sic* – Sicily; *Sp* – Spain; *SW* – Social War. The reference *BMC It* is to the page and entry number in *British Museum Catalogue of Greek Coins, Italy*.

1	*RC* p. 125	38	*R* 25	75	*It* 416	109	*It* 588
2	*AS* 2	39	*R* 43A	76	*cf.* Baarfeldt,	110	*It* 526
3	*BMC It* 62,1	40	*R* 45		*Die römische*	111	*It* 519
4	*RC* 1	41	*R* 180		*Goldmünzen-*	112	*It* 532
5	*RC* 14	42	*RC* 129		*prägungen,* 22,9	113	*It* 530
6	*BMC It* 48,1	43	*It* 78	77	*R* 585	114	*It* 649
7	*RC* 21	44	*R* 8	78	*R* 726	115	*It* 510
8	*RC* 26	45	*R* 9	79	*R* 663	116	*R* 1230
9	*BMC It* 51,1	46	*R* 13	80	*R* 717	117	*R* 1525
10	*RC* 28	47	*R* 228	81	*R* 776	118	*R* 1240
11	*BMC It* 53,1	48	*R* 234	82	*It* 550	119	*R* 1696A
12	*RC* 34	49	*R* 248	83	*R* 926	120	*R* 1674
13	*RC* 5	50	*R* 259	84	*R* 847	121	*R* 1127
14	*It (AG)* 1	51	*R* 266	85	*R* 886	122	*It* 735
15	*RC* 59	52	*R* 271	86	*R* 919	123	*It* 722
16	*RC* 63	53	*R* 276	87	*R* 881	124	*SW* 9
17	*RC* 68	54	*R* 185	88	*R* 902	125	*SW* 18
18	*RC* p. 130	55	*R* 188	89	*R* 971	126	*SW* 34
19	*RC* 49	56	*R* 189	90	*R* 969	127	*SW* 35
20	*RC* 70	57	*It* 60	91	*It* 540	128	*SW* p. 333
21	*RC* 45	58	*It* 242	92	*R* 1033	129	*SW* 48
22	*BMC It* 46,1	59	*It* 227	93	*R* 953	130	*R* 1858A
23	*RC* 83	60	*It* 244	94	*R* 917	131	*R* 2309
23	*RC* 111	61	*It* 180A	95	*R* 1139	132	*R* 2177
25	*RC* 108	62	*It* 236	96	*R* 1140	133	*R* 2192
26	*AG* 9	63	*It* 186A	97	*R* 1044	134	*R* 2322
27	*AG* 17	64	*It* 24	98	*R* 1035	135	*R* 2462A
28	*AG* 25	65	*It* 48	99	*R* 1035A	136	*R* 2372
29	*AG* 35	66	*It* 190A	100	*R* 1166	137	*R* 2464A
30	*AG* 46	67	*It* 195A	101	*R* 1176	138	*R* 2482
31	*AG* 55	68	*R* 287	102	*R* 1180	139	*R* 2483
32	*AG* 68	69	*R* 372A	103	*It* 555	140	*R* 2604
33	*RC* 101	70	*It* 265	104	*R* 1186	141	*E* 6
34	*RC* 75	71	*It* 169	105	*It* 493	142	*E* 1
35	*RC* 77	72	*It* 262	106	*It* 590	143	*E* 16
36	*R* 19	73	*R* 349	107	*It* 620	144	*R* 2657
37	*R* 22	74	*It* 116	108	*It* 632	145	*R* 2720

146	*R* 3143	190	*R* 3871	234	*Sp* 80	278	*E* 86
147	*R* 2839	191	*R* 3860	235	*R* 4023	279	*Af* 26
148	*G* 4	192	*R* 3861	236	*R* 4011	280	*Sic* 12
149	*Sp* 2	193	*R* 3864	237	*R* 4106	281	*Sic* 13
150	*R* 2905	194	*R* 3883	238	*R* 4114	282	*R* 4195
151	*R* 3005	195	*R* 3879	239	*R* 4123	283	*R* 4216
152	*R* 3156	196	*R* 3375	240	*R* 4125	284	*R* 4210
153	*R* 3159	197	*R* 3377	241	*Sp* 94	285	*R* 4205
154	*R* 3169	198	*R* 3891	242	*Sp* 103	286	*R* 4204
155	*R* 3188	199	*R* 3911A	243	*R* 4161	287	*G* 69
156	*R* 3207	200	*R* 3912	244	*R* 4136	288	*G* 60
157	*R* 3152	201	*R* 3940	245	*R* 4159	289	*G* 64
158	*R* 3293	202	*R* 3901	246	*R* 4173	290	*G* 80
159	*R* 3329	203	*R* 3928	247	*R* 4169	291	*E* 93
160	*R* 3324	204	*R* 3908	248	*R* 4146	292	*E* 94
161	*R* 3278	205	*R* 3837	249	*R* 4179	293	*E* 107
162	*R* 3340	206	*R* 4207	250	*R* 4176	294	*E* 132
163	*R* 3365	207	*G* 27	251	*R* 4203	295	*R* 4312
164	*R* 3312	208	*E* 24	252	*R* 4211	296	*R* 4317
165	*R* 3362	209	*Sic* 3	253	*R* 4223A	297	*G* 91
166	*R* 3370	210	*E* 23	254	*R* 4191A	298	*Af* 31
167	*R* 3523	211	*Sp* 62	255	*R* 4193A	299	*G* 73
168	*R* 3528	212	*Sp* 65	256	*E* 37	300	*Sp* 109
169	*R* 3660	213	*R* 3995	257	*G* 75	301	*E* 133
170	*R* 3642	214	*R* 3998	258	*G* 31	302	*E* 144
171	*R* 3648	215	*R* 3967	259	*G* 54	303	*E* 155
172	*R* 3652	216	*R* 3959	260	*R* 4255	304	*G* 100
173	*R* 3604	217	*R* 4004	261	*R* 4259	305	*G* 106
174	*R* 3609	218	*R* 4003	261	*R* 4258	306	*Sic* 15
175	*R* 3611	219	*R* 4030	263	*R* 4271	307	*Sic* 18
176	*R* 3612	220	*R* 4033	264	*R* 4276*	308	*Sic* 21
177	*R* 3613	221	*Sic* 5	265	*R* 4250	309	*NC* 1934,44
178	*R* 3615	222	*E* 32	266	*R* 4299	310	*E* 172
179	*R* 3617	223	*Af* 3	267	*G* 46	311	*Af* 32
180	*R* 3620	224	*Af* 6	268	*G* 47	312	*R* 4322
181	*R* 3625	225	*Af* 8	269	*E* 58	313	*R* 4333
182	*R* 3629	226	*Af* 13	270	*E* 52	314	*E* 174A
183	*R* 3512	227	*Af* 17	271	*E* 59	315	*E* 180
184	*R* 3415	228	*R* 4058	272	*E* 62	316	*E* 183
185	*R* 3820	229	*R* 4060	273	*E* 63	317	*E* 189
186	*R* 3824	230	*R* 4084	274	*E* 68	318	*E* 222
187	*R* 3828	231	*R* 4050	275	*E* 82	319	*Cyr* 1
188	*R* 3832	232	*Sp* 87	276	*E* 85A		
189	*E* 20	233	*Sp* 79	277	*E* 84		

Select Bibliography

M. von Bahrfeldt,
Die römische Goldmünzenprägung wahrend der Republik und unter Augustus, Halle, 1923.

M. H. Crawford,
Roman Republican Coinage, vols 1–2, Cambridge, 1975.

H. A. Grueber,
Coins of the Roman Republic in the British Museum, vols 1–3, London, 1910 (reprint 1970).

E. J. Haeberlin,
Aes Grave, Das Schwergeld Roms und Mittelitaliens, vols 1–2, Frankfurt-am-Main, 1910.

F. B. Marsh,
A History of the Roman World from 146 to 30 B.C., (Second edition, revised) London, 1953.

H. H. Scullard,
A History of the Roman World from 753 to 146 B.C., (Second edition, revised), London, 1951.

R. Stuart Poole,
A Catalogue of Greek Coins in the British Museum, Italy, London, 1873.

E. A. Sydenham,
The Coinage of the Roman Republic, London, 1952.

R. Thomsen,
Early Roman Coinage, vols 1–3, Copenhagen, 1957–62.

Indexes

I General

II Moneyers

This index includes both ordinary
moneying magistrates and other
officials who issued coins.